RESTORATIVE JUSTICE IN 1ST AND 2ND CORINTHIANS

Dr. Maxwell Shimba

Shimba Publishing, LLC

Printed in the United States of America

TABLE OF CONTENTS

PREFACE

Restorative justice is a concept deeply rooted in biblical teachings, particularly in the letters of Paul to the Corinthians. The first and second epistles to the Corinthians offer profound insights into the principles and practices of restorative justice. In these letters, Paul addresses various issues within the Corinthian church, emphasizing the importance of reconciliation, forgiveness, and the restoration of relationships.

In a world often dominated by retributive justice, where punishment is the primary response to wrongdoing, the biblical model of restorative justice presents an alternative that seeks healing and wholeness. Paul's approach in addressing conflicts, moral failures, and communal disputes in the Corinthian church provides a timeless blueprint for restorative practices in the Christian community and beyond.

This book aims to explore these principles in depth, providing a comprehensive understanding of how restorative justice is articulated and exemplified in these biblical texts. We will delve into the historical and cultural context of Corinth, examine specific passages where Paul's teachings on restorative justice are most evident, and consider practical applications for contemporary faith communities.

By understanding the biblical foundations of restorative justice, we can better appreciate its relevance and importance in our own lives. Through this exploration, readers will be encouraged to embrace restorative practices, fostering environments where reconciliation and healing can flourish. It is our hope that this book will inspire individuals and communities to seek justice that restores, reflecting the heart of God's redemptive work through Christ.

DR. MAXWELL SHIMBA

CHAPTER 01

UNDERSTANDING RESTORATIVE JUSTICE

Definition and Principles

Restorative justice is a framework for addressing harm and conflict that emphasizes healing, reconciliation, and the restoration of relationships. Unlike retributive justice, which focuses on punishment, restorative justice seeks to repair the damage caused by wrongdoing and to restore the relationships between the victim, the offender, and the community.

At its core, restorative justice is about addressing the needs of all parties involved in a conflict or harm: the victim, the offender, and the community. It recognizes that crime and wrongdoing cause harm that extends beyond the immediate incident, impacting relationships and community well-being.

Key Principles of Restorative Justice

1. Repairing Harm: The primary goal of restorative justice is to address the harm caused by wrongdoing. This

involves acknowledging the impact on the victim, taking responsibility for the actions, and making amends. The process focuses on healing for the victim and rehabilitation for the offender.

2. Involving Stakeholders: Restorative justice involves all stakeholders in the process of addressing harm. This includes the victim, the offender, their families, and members of the community. The aim is to create a dialogue where all voices are heard and valued.

3. Transforming Relationships: A significant aspect of restorative justice is the transformation of relationships. By focusing on reconciliation and mutual understanding, the process seeks to rebuild trust and foster positive relationships between the victim, the offender, and the community.

4. Accountability and Responsibility: Restorative justice emphasizes the offender's accountability and responsibility. Offenders are encouraged to understand the impact of their actions, take responsibility, and actively participate in making amends.

5. Reintegration: Reintegration is a critical component of restorative justice. It aims to restore offenders to their communities as contributing members, preventing recidivism and promoting long-term healing.

The Biblical Foundations of Restorative Justice

The principles of restorative justice are deeply embedded in the biblical narrative. Throughout the Bible, themes of forgiveness, reconciliation, and restoration are prevalent. The teachings of Jesus and the apostles, particularly Paul's letters, provide a robust framework for understanding and implementing restorative justice.

Old Testament Foundations

In the Old Testament, the laws given to Israel often included provisions for restitution and reconciliation. For example, the Law of Moses prescribed specific actions for restoring what was taken or damaged (Exodus 22:1-14). These laws emphasized making amends and restoring relationships rather than merely punishing the offender.

The concept of the Jubilee year (Leviticus 25) is another profound example. Every fifty years, debts were forgiven, slaves were freed, and land was returned to its original owners. This practice underscored the importance of restoration and the renewal of community ties.

New Testament Teachings

Jesus' teachings and actions further illustrate the principles of restorative justice. In the Sermon on the Mount, Jesus calls for reconciliation and peacemaking (Matthew 5:9, 23-24). He emphasizes the importance of forgiving others and seeking to restore relationships.

The parable of the prodigal son (Luke 15:11-32) is a powerful example of restorative justice. The father's response to his repentant son highlights forgiveness, acceptance, and the restoration of the relationship. Rather than punishment, the father offers love and reconciliation.

Paul's letters, particularly to the Corinthians, provide specific instructions and examples of how restorative justice can be practiced within the Christian community. His guidance on resolving conflicts, dealing with immorality, and fostering unity reflects a deep commitment to the principles of restorative justice.

Restorative Justice vs. Retributive Justice

To fully appreciate the concept of restorative justice, it is helpful to contrast it with retributive justice. Retributive justice is based on the idea that wrongdoing deserves punishment. It focuses on establishing guilt and administering penalties proportionate to the offense.

While retributive justice aims to deter future wrongdoing and uphold social order, it often fails to address the underlying harm and the needs of the victim. In contrast, restorative justice seeks to heal and restore, prioritizing the well-being of all parties involved.

Key Differences

1. Focus on Harm: Retributive justice focuses on the offense and the appropriate punishment. Restorative justice, on the other hand, focuses on the harm caused and how to repair it.

2. Role of the Victim: In retributive justice, the victim's role is often limited to providing evidence. Restorative justice involves the victim in the process, acknowledging their needs and perspectives.

3. Outcome Goals: Retributive justice aims to administer justice through punishment. Restorative justice aims to achieve healing, reconciliation, and the restoration of relationships.

4. Community Involvement: Retributive justice typically involves the state or legal system. Restorative justice actively involves the community in addressing harm and supporting both the victim and the offender.

Implementing restorative justice requires a shift in mindset and approach. It involves creating spaces where dialogue, understanding, and healing can occur. This can be achieved through various practices, such as mediation, community conferencing, and restorative circles.

Mediation

Mediation is a process where a neutral third party facilitates a conversation between the victim and the offender.

The goal is to foster understanding, address the harm, and agree on steps to make amends.

Community Conferencing

Community conferencing involves a broader group of stakeholders, including the victim, the offender, their families, and community members. The process encourages collective problem-solving and supports the reintegration of the offender into the community.

Restorative Circles

Restorative circles are a community-based approach where participants sit in a circle and engage in open dialogue. This process promotes mutual understanding, accountability, and the healing of relationships.

Restorative justice offers a transformative approach to addressing harm and conflict. By focusing on healing, reconciliation, and the restoration of relationships, it aligns with the biblical principles exemplified in Paul's letters to the Corinthians. Understanding and implementing restorative justice can lead to profound personal and communal transformation, reflecting the heart of the gospel message.

In the chapters that follow, we will delve deeper into the specific teachings of 1st and 2nd Corinthians, exploring how Paul's guidance on restorative justice can be applied in our lives and communities today. Through this exploration, we hope to provide a comprehensive understanding of restorative justice as a vital aspect of Christian faith and practice.

BIBLICAL FOUNDATIONS

The Bible provides numerous examples and teachings that align with the principles of restorative justice. From the laws given in the Old Testament to the teachings of Jesus and the apostles, the theme of restoration and reconciliation is pervasive. This chapter will explore these biblical foundations, illustrating how the concepts of healing, forgiveness, and the restoration of relationships are integral to the biblical narrative.

Old Testament Foundations

The Law of Moses

The Law of Moses, given to the Israelites, includes numerous provisions that emphasize restitution and restoration. For instance, in Exodus 22:1-14, various laws are outlined regarding theft and property damage. These laws require the offender to make restitution to the victim, often by repaying more than what was taken or damaged. This approach not only compensates the victim but also serves to restore the relationship between the offender and the community.

- Exodus 22:1: "Whoever steals an ox or a sheep and slaughters it or sells it must pay back five head of cattle for the ox and four sheep for the sheep."

- Exodus 22:14: "If anyone borrows an animal from their neighbor and it is injured or dies while the owner is not present, they must make restitution."

These laws reflect a deep concern for justice that goes beyond punishment, aiming to repair the harm caused and restore social harmony.

The Year of Jubilee

The concept of the Year of Jubilee, described in Leviticus 25, is another profound example of restorative justice in the Old Testament. Every fifty years, debts were forgiven, slaves were freed, and land was returned to its original owners. This practice ensured that long-term economic disparities did not become entrenched, and it provided a fresh start for those who had fallen into hardship.

- Leviticus 25:10: "Consecrate the fiftieth year and proclaim liberty throughout the land to all its inhabitants. It shall be a jubilee for you; each of you is to return to your family property and to your own clan."

The Year of Jubilee emphasized the importance of restoration and renewal, ensuring that relationships and communities were continually refreshed and revitalized.

Prophetic Calls for Justice

The prophets of the Old Testament frequently called for justice that encompassed restoration and reconciliation. Their messages often highlighted the need for social justice and the restoration of right relationships within the community.

- Micah 6:8: "He has shown you, O mortal, what is good. And what does the LORD require of you? To act justly and to love mercy and to walk humbly with your God."

Micah's call to act justly and love mercy underscores the holistic nature of biblical justice, which includes elements of restorative justice. The prophets consistently called the people to not only avoid wrongdoing but to actively seek the restoration of justice and mercy in their communities.

New Testament Teachings

The Teachings of Jesus

Jesus' teachings and actions provide a powerful foundation for restorative justice. Throughout his ministry, Jesus emphasized forgiveness, reconciliation, and the restoration of broken relationships.

- Matthew 5:23-24: "Therefore, if you are offering your gift at the altar and there remember that your brother or sister has something against you, leave your gift there in front of the altar. First, go and be reconciled to them; then come and offer your gift."

In this passage, Jesus highlights the importance of reconciliation over ritual. The priority is to restore relationships before engaging in religious practices, underscoring the value placed on interpersonal harmony.

The Parable of the Prodigal Son

The parable of the prodigal son (Luke 15:11-32) is a profound illustration of restorative justice. The story tells of a father who welcomes his repentant son back with open arms, restoring him to his place in the family despite his past mistakes.

- Luke 15:20: "But while he was still a long way off, his father saw him and was filled with compassion for him; he ran to his son, threw his arms around him and kissed him."

The father's response is a powerful example of forgiveness and restoration. Rather than focusing on punishment, the father's actions restore the son's dignity and place within the family, highlighting the principles of restorative justice.

Paul's Teachings

The apostle Paul's letters provide specific instructions and examples of how restorative justice can be practiced within the Christian community. In his letters to the

Corinthians, Paul addresses various issues and offers guidance on resolving conflicts and restoring relationships.

- 2 Corinthians 5:18-19: "All this is from God, who reconciled us to himself through Christ and gave us the ministry of reconciliation: that God was reconciling the world to himself in Christ, not counting people's sins against them. And he has committed to us the message of reconciliation."

Paul's emphasis on the ministry of reconciliation highlights the central role of restorative justice in the Christian faith. Believers are called to be agents of reconciliation, reflecting God's restorative work through Christ.

Case Studies in Biblical Restorative Justice

The Case of Zacchaeus

The story of Zacchaeus (Luke 19:1-10) provides a vivid example of restorative justice in action. Zacchaeus, a tax collector, experiences a transformative encounter with Jesus, leading to his decision to make restitution for his wrongs.

- Luke 19:8: "But Zacchaeus stood up and said to the Lord, 'Look, Lord! Here and now I give half of my possessions to the poor, and if I have cheated anybody out of anything, I will pay back four times the amount.'"

Zacchaeus' commitment to restitution reflects the principles of restorative justice, as he seeks to repair the harm caused by his actions and restore his relationship with the community.

The Corinthian Offender

In 2 Corinthians 2:5-11, Paul addresses the issue of a member of the Corinthian church who had caused significant harm. After the offender's repentance, Paul urges the community to forgive and comfort him, reaffirming their love for him.

- 2 Corinthians 2:7-8: "Now instead, you ought to forgive and comfort him, so that he will not be overwhelmed by excessive sorrow. I urge you, therefore, to reaffirm your love for him."

Paul's instructions reflect the principles of restorative justice, emphasizing forgiveness, comfort, and the reintegration of the offender into the community.

The biblical foundations of restorative justice are rich and multifaceted, encompassing laws, prophetic calls, teachings of Jesus, and the apostolic guidance of Paul. These examples and teachings illustrate the importance of healing, reconciliation, and the restoration of relationships. By understanding these biblical principles, we can better appreciate the depth and significance of restorative justice and its relevance for our lives and communities today.

In the following chapters, we will delve deeper into the specific teachings of 1st and 2nd Corinthians, exploring how Paul's guidance on restorative justice can be applied in contemporary faith communities. Through this exploration, we hope to provide a comprehensive understanding of restorative justice as a vital aspect of Christian faith and practice.

CHAPTER 02

CONTEXT OF 1ST AND 2ND CORINTHIANS

Historical and Cultural Background

To fully understand the concept of restorative justice in 1st and 2nd Corinthians, it is essential to grasp the historical and cultural context of Corinth in the first century. Corinth was a bustling, diverse city with significant social, economic, and moral challenges. This chapter explores the historical, cultural, and social backdrop of Corinth, providing insight into the environment in which Paul wrote his letters and the issues he addressed.

The City of Corinth

Geographical Significance

Corinth was strategically located on the narrow isthmus connecting the Greek mainland with the Peloponnesian peninsula. This location made it a major hub for trade and commerce, attracting a diverse population of merchants, sailors, and travelers from across the Roman Empire. The city's ports, Lechaeum on the Gulf of Corinth and Cenchreae on the Saronic Gulf facilitated extensive trade routes, contributing to its wealth and cosmopolitan character.

Economic Prosperity

Corinth was one of the wealthiest cities in the ancient world, known for its opulence and luxurious lifestyle. The city's prosperity was driven by its strategic location, which enabled it to control key trade routes and generate substantial revenue from commerce. This economic affluence, however, also led to significant social stratification, with stark contrasts between the wealthy elite and the poorer segments of the population.

Cultural Diversity

The population of Corinth was a melting pot of cultures, languages, and religions. This diversity brought a rich tapestry of traditions and customs but also led to various social and moral challenges. The city's cosmopolitan nature fostered a wide range of religious practices, including the worship of Greek, Roman, and Eastern deities. This pluralistic environment presented both opportunities and challenges for the early Christian community in Corinth.

Social and Moral Challenges

Idolatry and Pagan Worship

The prevalence of idolatry and pagan worship was a significant challenge for the Christian community in Corinth. Temples dedicated to various gods and goddesses, such as Aphrodite and Poseidon, were prominent features of the city. The Temple of Aphrodite, in particular, was infamous for its association with ritual prostitution, reflecting the moral decay that Paul addresses in his letters.

Sexual Immorality

Corinth was notorious for its sexual immorality, a reputation that was exacerbated by its association with the worship of Aphrodite. The city's licentious behavior posed a serious threat to the moral integrity of the Christian community. Paul addresses issues of sexual immorality directly in his letters, emphasizing the need for purity and holiness among believers.

- 1 Corinthians 6:18-20: "Flee from sexual immorality. All other sins a person commits are outside the body, but whoever sins sexually, sins against their own body. Do you not know that your bodies are temples of the Holy Spirit, who is in you, whom you have received from God? You are not your own; you were bought at a price. Therefore honor God with your bodies."

Social Stratification

The significant economic disparities in Corinth led to social stratification and tensions within the community. The wealthy elite often flaunted their status, while the poor struggled to survive. These divisions were evident in the church, as seen in the issues surrounding the Lord's Supper, where the wealthy members would feast while the poorer members went hungry.

- 1 Corinthians 11:20-22: "So then, when you come together, it is not the Lord's Supper you eat, for when you are eating, some of you go ahead with your own private suppers. As a result, one person remains hungry and another gets drunk. Don't you have homes to eat and drink in? Or do you despise the church of God by humiliating those who have nothing? What shall I say to you? Shall I praise you? Certainly not in this matter!"

The Corinthian Church

Founding of the Church

The church in Corinth was founded by the apostle Paul during his second missionary journey, around AD 50-51. Paul spent approximately 18 months in Corinth, preaching the gospel and establishing the Christian community. The initial converts were a diverse group, including Jews, Gentiles, and individuals from various social and economic backgrounds.

- Acts 18:1-4: "After this, Paul left Athens and went to Corinth. There he met a Jew named Aquila, a native of Pontus, who had recently come from Italy with his wife Priscilla, because Claudius had ordered all Jews to leave Rome. Paul went to see them, and because he was a tentmaker as they were, he stayed and worked with them. Every Sabbath he reasoned in the synagogue, trying to persuade Jews and Greeks."

Challenges and Issues

The diversity of the Corinthian church brought both vitality and challenges. The congregation faced various internal conflicts and moral issues that threatened its unity and witness. Key issues included divisions and factions, sexual immorality, lawsuits among believers, and misunderstandings about Christian doctrine and practice.

Divisions and Factions

One of the primary issues addressed by Paul in his letters is the divisions within the church. The Corinthians were aligning themselves with different leaders (Paul, Apollos, Cephas, and Christ), leading to factionalism and disunity.

- 1 Corinthians 1:10-12: "I appeal to you, brothers and sisters, in the name of our Lord Jesus Christ, that all of you agree with one another in what you say and that there be no divisions among you, but that you be perfectly united in mind and thought. My brothers and sisters, some from Chloe's household have informed me that there are quarrels among you. What I mean is this: One of you says, 'I follow Paul'; another, 'I follow Apollos'; another, 'I follow Cephas'; still another, 'I follow Christ.'"

Sexual Immorality

The moral laxity of the surrounding culture infiltrated the church, leading to serious cases of sexual immorality that Paul had to address firmly.

- 1 Corinthians 5:1-2: "It is actually reported that there is sexual immorality among you, and of a kind that even pagans do not tolerate: A man is sleeping with his father's wife. And you are proud! Shouldn't you rather have gone into mourning and have put out of your fellowship the man who has been doing this?"

Lawsuits Among Believers

Paul was also concerned about believers taking their disputes to secular courts rather than resolving them within the Christian community. This practice not only damaged the church's witness but also undermined the principles of restorative justice that Paul advocated.

- 1 Corinthians 6:1-6: "If any of you has a dispute with another, do you dare to take it before the ungodly for judgment instead of before the Lord's people? Or do you not know that the Lord's people will judge the world? And if you are to judge the world, are you not competent to judge trivial cases? Do you not know that we will judge angels? How much more the things of this life! Therefore, if you have disputes about such matters, do you ask for a ruling from those whose way of life is scorned in the church? I say this to shame you. Is it possible that there is nobody among you wise enough to judge a dispute between believers? But instead, one brother takes another to court—and this in front of unbelievers!"

Paul's Response and Guidance

Paul's letters to the Corinthians provide specific instructions and guidance for addressing these issues. His approach is deeply rooted in the principles of restorative justice, emphasizing reconciliation, healing, and the restoration of relationships.

Promoting Unity

To address the divisions within the church, Paul calls for unity and mutual respect. He reminds the Corinthians that they are all part of the body of Christ and should work together in harmony.

- 1 Corinthians 12:12-13: "Just as a body, though one, has many parts, but all its many parts form one body, so it is with Christ. For we were all baptized by one Spirit so as to form one body—whether Jews or Gentiles, slave or free—and we were all given the one Spirit to drink."

Addressing Moral Laxity

Paul takes a firm stance against sexual immorality, urging the church to take disciplinary action while also seeking the restoration of the offender. His goal is to maintain the moral integrity of the community and facilitate genuine repentance and reconciliation.

- 1 Corinthians 5:5: "Hand this man over to Satan for the destruction of the flesh, so that his spirit may be saved on the day of the Lord."

Encouraging Forgiveness and Reconciliation

In his second letter, Paul emphasizes the importance of forgiveness and reconciliation, particularly for those who have repented. He urges the church to reaffirm its love for the offender, highlighting the restorative aspect of church discipline.

- 2 Corinthians 2:7-8: "Now instead, you ought to forgive and comfort him, so that he will not be overwhelmed by excessive sorrow. I urge you, therefore, to reaffirm your love for him."

The historical and cultural context of Corinth provides a vital backdrop for understanding Paul's letters to the Corinthians. The challenges faced by the Corinthian church, including divisions, moral laxity, and social stratification, necessitated Paul's guidance and intervention. His responses, deeply rooted in the principles of restorative justice, offer timeless lessons for addressing conflict and fostering reconciliation within the Christian community.

In the subsequent chapters, we will delve deeper into specific teachings and passages from 1st and 2nd Corinthians, exploring how Paul's instructions can be applied to contemporary faith communities. Through this exploration, we aim to provide a comprehensive understanding of restorative justice as a vital

THE CORINTHIANS CHURCH

The church in Corinth was a vibrant but troubled community. Paul's letters to the Corinthians address various issues, including divisions, immorality, and misunderstandings about Christian doctrine and practice. This chapter delves into the life of the Corinthian church, exploring its strengths, weaknesses, and the challenges it faced. By understanding the specific issues Paul addressed, we can better appreciate the relevance of his teachings on restorative justice.

Founding of the Corinthian Church

Paul's Missionary Journey

The apostle Paul founded the church in Corinth during his second missionary journey, around AD 50-51. Arriving in Corinth, Paul initially stayed with Aquila and Priscilla, fellow tentmakers who had recently come from Italy. He began his ministry in the local synagogue, reasoning with Jews and Greeks every Sabbath.

- Acts 18:1-4: "After this, Paul left Athens and went to Corinth. There he met a Jew named Aquila, a native of Pontus, who had recently come from Italy with his wife Priscilla, because Claudius had ordered all Jews to leave Rome. Paul went to see them, and because he was a tentmaker as they were, he stayed and worked with them. Every Sabbath he reasoned in the synagogue, trying to persuade Jews and Greeks."

Establishing the Church

Paul's preaching in Corinth met with both success and opposition. When opposition from the Jewish community intensified, he shifted his focus to the Gentiles. He continued his ministry from the house of Titius Justus, a Gentile believer whose home was next to the synagogue. Many Corinthians, including Crispus, the synagogue leader, believed in the Lord and were baptized.

- Acts 18:7-8: "Then Paul left the synagogue and went next door to the house of Titius Justus, a worshiper of God.

Crispus, the synagogue leader, and his entire household believed in the Lord; and many of the Corinthians who heard Paul believed and were baptized."

Paul spent about 18 months in Corinth, teaching the word of God and establishing a strong Christian community. His time in Corinth laid the foundation for a church that would become both influential and problematic.

The Challenges of the Corinthian Church

Divisions and Factions

One of the most significant issues facing the Corinthian church was divisions and factions. The believers were aligning themselves with different leaders, creating discord and undermining the unity of the church.

- 1 Corinthians 1:10-12: "I appeal to you, brothers and sisters, in the name of our Lord Jesus Christ, that all of you agree with one another in what you say and that there be no divisions among you, but that you be perfectly united in mind and thought. My brothers and sisters, some from Chloe's household have informed me that there are quarrels among you. What I mean is this: One of you says, 'I follow Paul'; another, 'I follow Apollos'; another, 'I follow Cephas'; still another, 'I follow Christ.'"

Paul addresses this issue by emphasizing the importance of unity in Christ. He reminds the Corinthians that their allegiance should be to Christ alone and that human leaders are merely servants through whom they came to believe.

- 1 Corinthians 3:5-7: "What, after all, is Apollos? And what is Paul? Only servants, through whom you came to believe—as the Lord has assigned to each his task. I planted the seed, and Apollos watered it, but God has been making it grow. So neither the one who plants nor the one who waters is anything, but only God, who makes things grow."

Immorality and Church Discipline

Another major issue in the Corinthian church was sexual immorality. Corinth's reputation for moral laxity influenced the church, leading to significant moral failures among its members. Paul addresses a particularly egregious case in 1 Corinthians 5, where a man is reported to be in a relationship with his father's wife.

- 1 Corinthians 5:1-2: "It is actually reported that there is sexual immorality among you, and of a kind that even pagans do not tolerate: A man is sleeping with his father's wife. And you are proud! Shouldn't you rather have gone into mourning and have put out of your fellowship the man who has been doing this?"

Paul's response is firm: the church must expel the immoral brother to maintain its purity and integrity. However, his goal is not merely punitive but restorative. By removing the offender from the fellowship, Paul hopes the man will come to repentance and eventually be restored.

- 1 Corinthians 5:5: "Hand this man over to Satan for the destruction of the flesh, so that his spirit may be saved on the day of the Lord."

Lawsuits Among Believers

The Corinthian church also struggled with internal disputes, which some members were taking to secular courts rather than resolving within the church. Paul criticizes this practice, arguing that it undermines the church's witness and fails to embody the principles of Christian love and reconciliation.

- 1 Corinthians 6:1-6: "If any of you has a dispute with another, do you dare to take it before the ungodly for judgment instead of before the Lord's people? Or do you not know that the Lord's people will judge the world? And if you are to judge the world, are you not competent to judge trivial cases? Do you not know that we will judge angels? How much more the things of this life! Therefore, if you have disputes about such matters, do you ask for a ruling from those whose way of life is scorned in the church? I say this to shame you. Is it possible that there is nobody among you wise enough to judge a dispute between believers? But instead, one brother takes another to court—and this in front of unbelievers!"

Paul urges the Corinthians to resolve their disputes within the church, emphasizing the principles of forgiveness, reconciliation, and the restoration of relationships.

Misunderstandings About Doctrine

The Corinthian church also faced misunderstandings about various Christian doctrines and practices. Issues such as the proper conduct of the Lord's Supper, the use of spiritual gifts, and the resurrection of the dead were causing confusion and division.

The Lord's Supper

The Corinthians were misusing the Lord's Supper, turning it into a time of division and indulgence rather than a solemn remembrance of Christ's sacrifice. Paul addresses this issue in 1 Corinthians 11, calling the church to self-examination and proper observance of the sacrament.

- 1 Corinthians 11:20-22: "So then, when you come together, it is not the Lord's Supper you eat, for when you are eating, some of you go ahead with your own private suppers. As a result, one person remains hungry and another gets drunk. Don't you have homes to eat and drink in? Or do you despise the church of God by humiliating those who have nothing? What shall I say to you? Shall I praise you? Certainly not in this matter!"

Spiritual Gifts

The use and abuse of spiritual gifts were causing further divisions within the church. Paul dedicates a significant portion of his letter to teaching about the proper use of spiritual gifts, emphasizing that they should be used for the edification of the church and exercised in love.

- 1 Corinthians 12:4-7: "There are different kinds of gifts, but the same Spirit distributes them. There are different kinds of service, but the same Lord. There are different kinds of working, but in all of them and in everyone it is the same God at work. Now to each one the manifestation of the Spirit is given for the common good."

The Resurrection

Misunderstandings about the resurrection were also causing confusion and leading some to question the fundamental tenets of the faith. Paul addresses these concerns in 1 Corinthians 15, providing a detailed explanation of the resurrection of the dead and its significance for Christian hope.

- 1 Corinthians 15:12-14: "But if it is preached that Christ has been raised from the dead, how can some of you say that there is no resurrection of the dead? If there is no resurrection of the dead, then not even Christ has been raised. And if Christ has not been raised, our preaching is useless and so is your faith."

Paul's Response and Guidance

Promoting Unity and Love

Throughout his letters, Paul emphasizes the importance of unity and love within the church. He calls the Corinthians to put aside their divisions and to seek the common good, using their gifts and resources to build up the body of Christ.

- 1 Corinthians 13:1-3: "If I speak in the tongues of men or of angels, but do not have love, I am only a resounding gong or a clanging cymbal. If I have the gift of prophecy and can fathom all mysteries and all knowledge, and if I have a faith that can move mountains, but do not have love, I am nothing. If I give all I possess to the poor and give over my body to hardship that I may boast, but do not have love, I gain nothing."

Addressing Immorality with a Restorative Approach

Paul's approach to addressing immorality is both firm and restorative. He calls for decisive action to maintain the church's purity but always with the aim of repentance and restoration.

- 2 Corinthians 2:6-8: "The punishment inflicted on him by the majority is sufficient. Now instead, you ought to forgive and comfort him, so that he will not be overwhelmed by excessive sorrow. I urge you, therefore, to reaffirm your love for him."

Encouraging Proper Conduct and Doctrine

Paul provides clear instructions for proper conduct and doctrine, addressing specific issues and guiding the Corinthians toward a deeper understanding of their faith. His teachings on the Lord's Supper, spiritual gifts, and the resurrection are intended to bring clarity and unity to the church.

- 1 Corinthians 14:26: "What then shall we say, brothers and sisters? When you come together, each of you has a hymn, or a word of instruction, a revelation, a tongue or an interpretation. Everything must be done so that the church may be built up."

The Corinthian church was a vibrant but troubled community, facing numerous challenges that threatened its unity and integrity. Paul's letters address these issues with a combination of firm correction and compassionate guidance, emphasizing the principles of restorative justice. By promoting unity, addressing immorality with a restorative approach, and encouraging proper conduct and doctrine, Paul sought to build a community that reflected the love and reconciliation found in Christ.

Understanding the specific issues and challenges faced by the Corinthian church helps us appreciate the relevance of Paul's teachings on restorative justice. In the following chapters, we will delve deeper into specific passages from 1st and 2nd Corinthians, exploring how Paul's instructions can be applied to contemporary faith communities. Through this exploration, we aim to provide a comprehensive understanding of restorative justice as a vital aspect of Christian faith and practice.

CHAPTER 03

RESTORATIVE JUSTICE IN 1ST CORINTHIANS

Addressing Division and Factionalism (1 Corinthians 1-4)

Paul begins his first letter to the Corinthians by addressing the divisions within the church. He emphasizes the importance of unity and reconciliation, urging the community to focus on Christ rather than human leaders. This chapter explores how Paul applies principles of restorative justice to address division and factionalism in the Corinthian church, offering insights for contemporary application.

The Problem of Division

The Corinthian church was plagued by divisions and factionalism. Members of the church were aligning themselves with different leaders, creating discord and undermining the unity of the community.

- 1 Corinthians 1:10-12: "I appeal to you, brothers and sisters, in the name of our Lord Jesus Christ, that all of you agree with one another in what you say and that there be no divisions among you, but that you be perfectly united in mind and thought. My brothers and sisters, some from Chloe's household have informed me that there are quarrels among you. What I mean is this: One of you says, 'I follow Paul'; another, 'I follow Apollos'; another, 'I follow Cephas'; still another, 'I follow Christ.'"

Paul's appeal is a call for unity and mutual respect. He addresses the root cause of the divisions: the Corinthians' misplaced loyalty to human leaders rather than to Christ.

Theological Foundation for Unity

Paul provides a theological foundation for unity by reminding the Corinthians that Christ is the source of their salvation and the head of the church. Human leaders are merely servants through whom they came to believe.

- 1 Corinthians 3:5-7: "What, after all, is Apollos? And what is Paul? Only servants, through whom you came to believe—as the Lord has assigned to each his task. I planted the seed, and Apollos watered it, but God has been making it grow. So neither the one who plants nor the one who waters is anything, but only God, who makes things grow."

By emphasizing that God is the one who causes growth, Paul redirects the Corinthians' focus from human leaders to God. This theological perspective is essential for fostering unity and reconciliation within the church.

The Role of Servant Leadership

Paul also addresses the issue of leadership by redefining what it means to be a leader in the Christian community. He emphasizes that true leadership is characterized by servanthood and humility.

- 1 Corinthians 4:1-2: "This, then, is how you ought to regard us: as servants of Christ and as those entrusted with the mysteries God has revealed. Now it is required that those who have been given a trust must prove faithful."

By presenting himself and other leaders as servants, Paul challenges the Corinthians to adopt a humble attitude and to value faithfulness over personal allegiance. This perspective is crucial for overcoming division and fostering a culture of mutual respect and collaboration.

Addressing the Root Causes of Division

Paul identifies several root causes of division within the Corinthian church, including pride, worldly wisdom, and a lack of spiritual maturity. He addresses these issues directly, offering guidance on how to overcome them.

Pride and Boasting

Pride and boasting were significant factors contributing to the divisions in Corinth. Paul warns against these attitudes, reminding the Corinthians that their status and achievements are gifts from God.

- 1 Corinthians 1:28-31: "God chose the lowly things of this world and the despised things—and the things that are not—to nullify the things that are, so that no one may boast before him. It is because of him that you are in Christ Jesus, who has become for us wisdom from God—that is, our righteousness, holiness and redemption. Therefore, as it is written: 'Let the one who boasts boast in the Lord.'"

By emphasizing that all boasting should be in the Lord, Paul seeks to eliminate the pride and arrogance that fuel division and to promote a spirit of humility and gratitude.

Worldly Wisdom vs. Godly Wisdom

Another root cause of division was the Corinthians' reliance on worldly wisdom rather than godly wisdom. Paul contrasts the two, highlighting the superiority of God's wisdom.

- 1 Corinthians 2:6-8: "We do, however, speak a message of wisdom among the mature, but not the wisdom of this age or of the rulers of this age, who are coming to nothing. No, we declare God's wisdom, a mystery that has been hidden and that God destined for our glory before time began."

Paul's emphasis on godly wisdom encourages the Corinthians to seek understanding and guidance from God rather than from worldly philosophies. This shift in focus is essential for overcoming division and fostering spiritual maturity.

Spiritual Maturity

Paul also addresses the issue of spiritual maturity, or the lack thereof, within the Corinthian church. He encourages the Corinthians to grow in their faith and understanding, moving beyond petty disputes and divisions.

- 1 Corinthians 3:1-3: "Brothers and sisters, I could not address you as people who live by the Spirit but as people who are still worldly—mere infants in Christ. I gave you milk, not solid food, for you were not yet ready for it. Indeed, you are still not ready. You are still worldly. For since there is jealousy and quarreling among you, are you not worldly? Are you not acting like mere humans?"

By calling the Corinthians to spiritual maturity, Paul seeks to address the underlying issues that contribute to division and to promote a culture of growth and unity within the church.

Practical Steps for Reconciliation

In addition to addressing the root causes of division, Paul offers practical steps for reconciliation. These steps are grounded in the principles of restorative justice and are aimed at fostering healing and unity within the church.

Emphasizing Common Identity in Christ

Paul emphasizes the common identity of all believers in Christ, reminding the Corinthians that they are one body, united by the Spirit.

- 1 Corinthians 12:12-13: "Just as a body, though one, has many parts, but all its many parts form one body, so it is with Christ. For we were all baptized by one Spirit so as to form one body—whether Jews or Gentiles, slave or free—and we were all given the one Spirit to drink."

By focusing on their shared identity in Christ, Paul encourages the Corinthians to see each other as brothers and sisters, fostering a spirit of unity and mutual support.

Encouraging Mutual Respect and Honor

Paul calls the Corinthians to honor and respect one another, recognizing the value and contributions of each member of the community.

- 1 Corinthians 12:24-26: "But God has put the body together, giving greater honor to the parts that lacked it, so that there should be no division in the body, but that its parts should have equal concern for each other. If one part suffers, every part suffers with it; if one part is honored, every part rejoices with it."

By promoting mutual respect and concern, Paul seeks to eliminate the divisions and factions that have plagued the church and to foster a culture of solidarity and support.

Promoting Love as the Foundation

Above all, Paul emphasizes love as the foundation for all relationships and actions within the church. In his famous discourse on love in 1 Corinthians 13, he highlights the centrality of love for maintaining unity and promoting restorative justice.

- 1 Corinthians 13:1-3: "If I speak in the tongues of men or of angels, but do not have love, I am only a resounding gong or a clanging cymbal. If I have the gift of prophecy and can fathom all mysteries and all knowledge, and if I have a faith that can move mountains, but do not have love, I am nothing. If I give all I possess to the poor and give over my body to hardship that I may boast, but do not have love, I gain nothing."

By calling the Corinthians to love one another, Paul lays the foundation for a community that embodies the principles of restorative justice, where relationships are healed, and unity is preserved.

In addressing the divisions and factionalism within the Corinthian church, Paul applies the principles of restorative justice to promote unity and reconciliation. By emphasizing the importance of focusing on Christ, adopting a humble and servant-hearted attitude, addressing the root causes of division, and promoting practical steps for reconciliation, Paul provides a blueprint for overcoming discord and fostering a culture of mutual respect and love.

Understanding Paul's approach to addressing division and factionalism in 1 Corinthians offers valuable insights for contemporary faith communities. By applying these principles, churches today can work towards healing and unity, reflecting the heart of restorative justice and the reconciling work of Christ.

In the following chapters, we will continue to explore Paul's teachings on restorative justice in 1st and 2nd Corinthians, examining how his instructions can be applied to address various issues within the church and promote a culture of reconciliation and healing. Through this exploration, we aim to provide a comprehensive understanding of restorative justice as a vital aspect of Christian faith and practice.

SEXUAL IMMORALITY AND DISCIPLINE (1 CORINTHIANS 5)

In 1 Corinthians 5, Paul addresses a case of egregious sexual immorality within the Corinthian church and outlines steps for the community to take. His approach reflects restorative justice principles, aiming not only to address the wrongdoing but also to restore the offender and protect the community. This chapter explores Paul's guidance on handling sexual immorality and church discipline, highlighting the restorative aspects of his instructions.

The Problem of Sexual Immorality

The Specific Case

Paul confronts a specific case of sexual immorality involving a man who is in a relationship with his father's wife. This situation was considered scandalous, even by the standards of the surrounding pagan culture.

- 1 Corinthians 5:1-2: "It is actually reported that there is sexual immorality among you, and of a kind that even pagans do not tolerate: A man is sleeping with his father's wife. And you are proud! Shouldn't you rather have gone into mourning and have put out of your fellowship the man who has been doing this?"

Paul is shocked not only by the sin itself but also by the Corinthian church's complacency and pride regarding the situation. He expects the church to be in mourning over such a grievous sin and to take appropriate action to address it.

The Community's Responsibility

Paul emphasizes the responsibility of the entire church community in addressing the sin. He calls for collective action to remove the offender from their fellowship, highlighting the communal nature of discipline and accountability.

- 1 Corinthians 5:4-5: "So when you are assembled and I am with you in spirit, and the power of our Lord Jesus is present, hand this man over to Satan for the destruction of the flesh, so that his spirit may be saved on the day of the Lord."

Paul's directive to "hand this man over to Satan" indicates a form of excommunication, removing the individual from the protective sphere of the church community. This action is intended not as a final judgment but as a means to bring the offender to repentance and eventual restoration.

Principles of Restorative Justice

Addressing the Wrongdoing

Paul's primary concern is to address the wrongdoing and its impact on the church. By removing the offender from the community, Paul seeks to prevent further harm and to uphold the moral integrity of the church.

- 1 Corinthians 5:6-7: "Your boasting is not good. Don't you know that a little yeast leavens the whole batch of dough? Get rid of the old yeast, so that you may be a new unleavened batch—as you really are. For Christ, our Passover lamb, has been sacrificed."

Paul uses the metaphor of yeast to illustrate how unchecked sin can permeate and corrupt the entire community. Addressing the wrongdoing is essential to maintaining the purity and health of the church.

Protecting the Community

Paul's instructions also aim to protect the community from the corrosive effects of sin. By taking decisive action, the church demonstrates its commitment to holiness and sets a standard for moral behavior.

- 1 Corinthians 5:11: "But now I am writing to you that you must not associate with anyone who claims to be a brother or sister but is sexually immoral or greedy, an idolater or slanderer, a drunkard or swindler. Do not even eat with such people."

This separation serves as a protective measure, preventing the normalization of sinful behavior and reinforcing the church's identity as a holy and distinct community.

Restoring the Offender

While Paul's immediate directive is to remove the offender, his ultimate goal is the restoration of the individual. The disciplinary action is intended to bring the offender to a point of repentance, leading to their spiritual salvation.

- 1 Corinthians 5:5: "Hand this man over to Satan for the destruction of the flesh, so that his spirit may be saved on the day of the Lord."

The phrase "destruction of the flesh" can be understood as a reference to the breaking down of sinful behaviors and attitudes, paving the way for genuine repentance and transformation. The hope is that, through this process, the offender will be saved and eventually restored to the community.

The Broader Implications for Church Discipline

A Balanced Approach

Paul's approach to church discipline balances justice with mercy, aiming to address wrongdoing while also seeking the offender's restoration. This balanced approach is a hallmark of restorative justice, which prioritizes healing and reconciliation over mere punishment.

Maintaining Moral Integrity

The case in 1 Corinthians 5 underscores the importance of maintaining moral integrity within the church. Paul's instructions remind us that the church must take sin seriously, addressing it decisively to preserve the community's holiness and witness.

Encouraging Repentance and Restoration

Paul's ultimate goal in church discipline is to encourage repentance and restoration. By creating an environment where sin is confronted and repentance is encouraged, the church can foster a culture of accountability, healing, and spiritual growth.

Practical Applications for Contemporary Churches

Establishing Clear Guidelines

Contemporary churches can learn from Paul's approach by establishing clear guidelines for addressing sin and implementing church discipline. These guidelines should be rooted in biblical principles and emphasize both justice and restoration.

Promoting a Culture of Accountability

Churches should promote a culture of accountability where members are encouraged to uphold moral standards and support one another in their spiritual journeys. This includes providing resources for repentance and restoration, such as counseling and support groups.

Balancing Justice and Mercy

In implementing church discipline, it is crucial to balance justice and mercy. Disciplinary actions should aim to protect the community and address wrongdoing while also seeking the offender's repentance and restoration.

In 1 Corinthians 5, Paul addresses a case of sexual immorality with a response that reflects restorative justice principles. His approach aims to address the wrongdoing, protect the community, and restore the offender. By emphasizing both justice and mercy, Paul provides a framework for church discipline that prioritizes healing and reconciliation.

Understanding Paul's guidance on handling sexual immorality and church discipline offers valuable insights for contemporary faith communities. By applying these principles, churches today can create environments where sin is confronted, repentance is encouraged, and relationships are restored.

In the following chapters, we will continue to explore Paul's teachings on restorative justice in 1st and 2nd Corinthians, examining how his instructions can be applied to address various issues within the church and promote a culture of reconciliation and healing. Through this exploration, we aim to provide a comprehensive

understanding of restorative justice as a vital aspect of Christian faith and practice.

LAWSUITS AMONG BELIEVERS (1 CORINTHIANS 6)

In 1 Corinthians 6, Paul criticizes the Corinthians for taking their disputes to secular courts. Instead, he advocates for resolving conflicts within the community, emphasizing reconciliation and restoration. This chapter explores Paul's instructions regarding lawsuits among believers, highlighting the principles of restorative justice that underlie his guidance.

The Problem of Lawsuits Among Believers

Taking Disputes to Secular Courts

The Corinthians were taking their disputes to secular courts rather than resolving them within the church. Paul is deeply concerned about this practice, as it undermines the church's witness and fails to embody the principles of Christian love and reconciliation.

- 1 Corinthians 6:1: "If any of you has a dispute with another, do you dare to take it before the ungodly for judgment instead of before the Lord's people?"

Paul's rhetorical question emphasizes his shock and disapproval. He finds it inappropriate for believers, who are part of a community founded on the teachings of Christ, to seek judgment from those outside the faith.

The Implications for the Church

By taking their disputes to secular courts, the Corinthians were not only exposing their internal conflicts to the public but also failing to demonstrate the transformative power of the gospel in resolving conflicts. This practice could damage the church's reputation and hinder its mission.

- 1 Corinthians 6:6: "But instead, one brother takes another to court—and this in front of unbelievers!"

Paul's concern is that such actions bring disgrace to the church and contradict the message of reconciliation and unity that the gospel proclaims.

Principles of Restorative Justice

Seeking Resolution Within the Community

Paul advocates for resolving disputes within the Christian community, emphasizing that believers should be capable of judging matters among themselves. This approach aligns with restorative justice principles, which prioritize reconciliation and restoration over retribution and adversarial proceedings.

- 1 Corinthians 6:2-3: "Or do you not know that the Lord's people will judge the world? And if you are to judge the world, are you not competent to judge trivial cases? Do you not know that we will judge angels? How much more the things of this life!"

Paul's argument is that the church, endowed with divine wisdom and the teachings of Christ, should be fully equipped to handle disputes internally. This perspective reinforces the idea that the community is responsible for maintaining justice and harmony among its members.

The Role of the Community in Conflict Resolution

In advocating for the internal resolution of disputes, Paul highlights the community's role in conflict resolution. He envisions a community where members actively work towards reconciliation and restoration, guided by the principles of love and mutual respect.

- 1 Corinthians 6:5: "I say this to shame you. Is it possible that there is nobody among you wise enough to judge a dispute between believers?"

Paul's rhetorical question challenges the Corinthians to rise to the occasion, using their collective wisdom and spiritual maturity to resolve conflicts.

Prioritizing Reconciliation Over Retaliation

Paul's approach prioritizes reconciliation and the restoration of relationships over retaliation and winning legal battles. He encourages believers to endure wrongs and seek peace, reflecting the teachings of Jesus on forgiveness and love.

- 1 Corinthians 6:7-8: "The very fact that you have lawsuits among you means you have been completely defeated already. Why not rather be wronged? Why not rather be cheated? Instead, you yourselves cheat and do wrong, and you do this to your brothers and sisters."

Paul's words emphasize that the pursuit of legal victories often results in spiritual defeat. He advocates for a higher standard of conduct, where believers prioritize reconciliation and the well-being of the community over personal grievances.

Practical Steps for Resolving Disputes

Establishing a Process for Conflict Resolution

To implement Paul's guidance, churches need to establish clear processes for resolving disputes within the community. These processes should be rooted in biblical principles and designed to facilitate reconciliation and restoration.

Mediation and Arbitration

Mediation and arbitration are practical methods for resolving disputes within the church. In mediation, a neutral third party facilitates a dialogue between the disputing parties, helping them reach a mutually agreeable resolution.

Arbitration involves a neutral party making a binding decision based on the evidence and arguments presented.

- Matthew 18:15-17: "If your brother or sister sins, go and point out their fault, just between the two of you. If they listen to you, you have won them over. But if they will not listen, take one or two others along, so that 'every matter may be established by the testimony of two or three witnesses.' If they still refuse to listen, tell it to the church; and if they refuse to listen even to the church, treat them as you would a pagan or a tax collector."

Jesus' instructions in Matthew 18 provide a framework for mediation and arbitration within the church, emphasizing the importance of resolving conflicts privately and progressively involving the community if necessary.

Encouraging Forgiveness and Reconciliation

Churches should cultivate a culture of forgiveness and reconciliation, encouraging members to prioritize these values in their interactions. This involves teaching and modeling the principles of restorative justice, highlighting the importance of repairing relationships and fostering unity.

- Colossians 3:13: "Bear with each other and forgive one another if any of you has a grievance against someone. Forgive as the Lord forgave you."

By emphasizing forgiveness, churches can help members move past conflicts and work toward genuine reconciliation.

Providing Support and Guidance

To effectively resolve disputes, churches should provide support and guidance to those involved in conflicts. This includes offering counseling, mentoring, and educational resources that equip members to handle disputes in a healthy and constructive manner.

Counseling and Pastoral Care

Counseling and pastoral care play a crucial role in supporting individuals involved in conflicts. Trained counselors and pastors can provide guidance, mediation, and emotional support, helping parties navigate their disputes and work toward resolution.

Educational Resources

Churches should also offer educational resources on conflict resolution and restorative justice. These resources can include workshops, seminars, and Bible studies that teach biblical principles and practical skills for resolving conflicts and fostering reconciliation.

The Broader Implications for the Church

Maintaining a Strong Witness

By resolving disputes internally and demonstrating a commitment to reconciliation, the church maintains a strong witness to the surrounding community. This approach showcases the transformative power of the gospel and the unique character of the Christian community.

Fostering a Culture of Peace

Implementing restorative justice principles in conflict resolution helps foster a culture of peace within the church. This culture is characterized by mutual respect, empathy, and a commitment to resolving conflicts in a way that honors God and strengthens relationships.

Encouraging Spiritual Growth

Resolving disputes within the community encourages spiritual growth by challenging members to practice forgiveness, humility, and love. This process helps individuals grow in their faith and develop deeper relationships with one another and with God.

In 1 Corinthians 6, Paul criticizes the Corinthians for taking their disputes to secular courts and advocates for resolving conflicts within the community. His approach reflects the principles of restorative justice, emphasizing reconciliation and restoration over retribution. By seeking resolution within the church, prioritizing reconciliation, and providing practical steps for conflict resolution, Paul offers a framework for handling disputes that promotes unity and reflects the heart of the gospel.

Understanding Paul's guidance on lawsuits among believers provides valuable insights for contemporary faith communities. By applying these principles, churches today can create environments where conflicts are resolved constructively, relationships are restored, and the community's witness is strengthened.

In the following chapters, we will continue to explore Paul's teachings on restorative justice in 1st and 2nd Corinthians, examining how his instructions can be applied to address various issues within the church and promote a culture of reconciliation and healing. Through this exploration, we aim to provide a comprehensive understanding of restorative justice as a vital aspect of Christian faith and practice.

THE LORD'S SUPPER (1 CORINTHIANS 11)

The improper observance of the Lord's Supper was a significant issue within the Corinthian church. Paul addresses this problem in 1 Corinthians 11, emphasizing the need for self-examination and mutual respect. His instructions highlight the communal and restorative nature of the Lord's

Supper, underscoring its importance in fostering unity and reconciliation within the Christian community.

The Problem of Improper Observance

Divisions and Inequality

In the Corinthian church, the Lord's Supper had become a source of division and inequality rather than a unifying practice. The wealthier members of the church were indulging in excess, while the poorer members were left hungry and humiliated.

- 1 Corinthians 11:17-22: "In the following directives I have no praise for you, for your meetings do more harm than good. In the first place, I hear that when you come together as a church, there are divisions among you, and to some extent, I believe it. No doubt there have to be differences among you to show which of you have God's approval. So then, when you come together, it is not the Lord's Supper you eat, for when you are eating, some of you go ahead with your own private suppers. As a result, one person remains hungry and another gets drunk. Don't you have homes to eat and drink in? Or do you despise the church of God by humiliating those who have nothing? What shall I say to you? Shall I praise you? Certainly not in this matter!"

Paul's rebuke highlights the seriousness of the situation. The improper observance of the Lord's Supper was not only disrespectful but also detrimental to the unity and integrity of the church.

The Need for Self-Examination

Paul calls for self-examination as an essential aspect of participating in the Lord's Supper. He emphasizes that individuals must reflect on their attitudes and behaviors, ensuring they approach the sacrament with the right heart and mind.

- 1 Corinthians 11:27-29: "So then, whoever eats the bread or drinks the cup of the Lord in an unworthy manner will be guilty of sinning against the body and blood of the Lord. Everyone ought to examine themselves before they eat of the bread and drink from the cup. For those who eat and drink without discerning the body of Christ eat and drink judgment on themselves."

Self-examination involves recognizing one's own shortcomings, seeking forgiveness, and committing to a life that honors Christ and the community.

The Communal Nature of the Lord's Supper

Remembering Christ's Sacrifice

The Lord's Supper is a communal practice that centers on remembering and proclaiming Christ's sacrificial death. Paul reminds the Corinthians of the institution of the Lord's Supper and its significance.

- 1 Corinthians 11:23-26: "For I received from the Lord what I also passed on to you: The Lord Jesus, on the night he was betrayed, took bread, and when he had given thanks, he broke it and said, 'This is my body, which is for you; do this in remembrance of me.' In the same way, after supper he took the cup, saying, 'This cup is the new covenant in my blood; do this, whenever you drink it, in remembrance of me.' For whenever you eat this bread and drink this cup, you proclaim the Lord's death until he comes."

By focusing on Christ's sacrifice, the community is reminded of the love and grace that binds them together. This shared remembrance fosters a sense of unity and mutual respect.

Fostering Unity and Mutual Respect

The Lord's Supper is intended to be a unifying practice that brings believers together as one body. Paul's instructions emphasize the importance of approaching the sacrament with an attitude of humility, respect, and love for one another.

- 1 Corinthians 11:33-34: "So then, my brothers and sisters, when you gather to eat, you should all eat together. Anyone who is hungry should eat something at home, so that when you meet together it may not result in judgment."

Paul encourages the Corinthians to wait for one another and to ensure that everyone is included and respected. This approach reflects the principles of restorative justice, promoting equality and communal harmony.

The Restorative Nature of the Lord's Supper

Healing and Reconciliation

The Lord's Supper is not only a time for remembrance but also a time for healing and reconciliation. By examining oneself and seeking forgiveness, individuals can restore their relationship with God and with each other.

- 1 Corinthians 11:28: "Everyone ought to examine themselves before they eat of the bread and drink from the cup."

This self-examination and subsequent repentance create an opportunity for personal and communal healing, fostering a sense of restoration and renewal within the community.

Preventing Judgment and Discipline

Paul warns the Corinthians that improper observance of the Lord's Supper can lead to judgment and discipline. However, he also provides a pathway to avoid such consequences through self-examination and proper conduct.

- 1 Corinthians 11:31-32: "But if we were more discerning with regard to ourselves, we would not come under such judgment. Nevertheless, when we are judged in this way by the Lord, we are being disciplined so that we will not be finally condemned with the world."

By taking the time to reflect and correct their behavior, the Corinthians can prevent divine judgment and experience the restorative benefits of the Lord's Supper.

Practical Applications for Contemporary Churches

Promoting Proper Observance

Contemporary churches can learn from Paul's instructions by promoting proper observance of the Lord's Supper. This includes teaching the significance of the sacrament, encouraging self-examination, and fostering an environment of mutual respect and unity.

Education and Instruction

Church leaders should provide education and instruction on the theological and practical aspects of the Lord's Supper. This can include sermons, Bible studies, and written resources that help congregants understand the importance of approaching the sacrament with the right heart and mind.

Encouraging Self-Examination

Churches should create opportunities for self-examination and reflection before participating in the Lord's

Supper. This can include moments of silence, guided prayers, and personal reflection time during the service.

Fostering Unity and Inclusion

Churches should ensure that the Lord's Supper is a unifying practice that includes all members of the community. This involves addressing any barriers to participation, such as socioeconomic differences, and promoting a culture of mutual respect and love.

Creating a Culture of Mutual Respect

To foster a culture of mutual respect, churches should emphasize the communal and restorative nature of the Lord's Supper. This includes addressing any practices or attitudes that may lead to division or inequality and promoting behaviors that reflect the principles of restorative justice.

Addressing Inequality and Division

Churches should be vigilant in addressing any forms of inequality or division within the community. This can include addressing economic disparities, social hierarchies, and any other factors that may hinder the unity of the church.

Promoting Inclusive Practices

Inclusive practices can help ensure that all members feel valued and respected during the Lord's Supper. This can include providing for the needs of those with dietary restrictions, ensuring accessibility for individuals with disabilities, and creating a welcoming environment for all.

The Broader Implications for the Church

Reflecting Christ's Love and Sacrifice

The proper observance of the Lord's Supper reflects Christ's love and sacrifice, demonstrating the transformative power of the gospel. By approaching the sacrament with the right heart and mind, the church can embody the principles of restorative justice and foster a sense of unity and reconciliation.

Strengthening the Community

Proper observance of the Lord's Supper strengthens the community by promoting healing, reconciliation, and mutual respect. This practice helps build a stronger, more cohesive church that can effectively witness to the love and grace of Christ.

Encouraging Spiritual Growth

Participating in the Lord's Supper with an attitude of self-examination and humility encourages spiritual growth. This process helps individuals develop a deeper relationship with God and fosters a sense of accountability and responsibility within the community.

In 1 Corinthians 11, Paul addresses the improper observance of the Lord's Supper, emphasizing the need for self-examination and mutual respect. His instructions highlight the communal and restorative nature of the sacrament, underscoring its importance in fostering unity and reconciliation within the Christian community.

Understanding Paul's guidance on the Lord's Supper provides valuable insights for contemporary faith communities. By promoting proper observance, encouraging self-examination, and fostering a culture of mutual respect, churches today can create environments where the Lord's Supper serves as a unifying and restorative practice.

In the following chapters, we will continue to explore Paul's teachings on restorative justice in 1st and 2nd Corinthians, examining how his instructions can be applied to address various issues within the church and promote a culture of reconciliation and healing. Through this exploration, we aim to provide a comprehensive understanding of restorative justice as a vital aspect of Christian faith and practice.

CHAPTER 04

RESTORATIVE JUSTICE IN 2ND CORINTHIANS

The Offender's Reconciliation (2 Corinthians 2:5-11)

Paul's second letter to the Corinthians continues the theme of restorative justice, particularly in 2 Corinthians 2:5-11, where he urges the community to forgive and comfort a repentant offender, reaffirming their love for him. This chapter explores Paul's guidance on the reconciliation of an offender, emphasizing the principles of forgiveness, comfort, and restoration.

The Context of the Offense

The Situation

In his first letter to the Corinthians, Paul addressed a case of serious misconduct involving a member of the church. The individual's actions had caused significant harm to the community, leading Paul to recommend disciplinary measures. The offender was likely the same individual mentioned in 1 Corinthians 5, who was involved in an egregious act of immorality.

- 1 Corinthians 5:1-2: "It is actually reported that there is sexual immorality among you, and of a kind that even pagans do not tolerate: A man is sleeping with his father's wife. And you are proud! Shouldn't you rather have gone into mourning and have put out of your fellowship the man who has been doing this?"

The church took Paul's advice seriously, resulting in the offender's exclusion from the community. However, by the time Paul writes his second letter, the offender has repented and sought reconciliation with the church.

The Need for Forgiveness and Reconciliation

Paul recognizes the need for the church to forgive the repentant offender and to restore him to the community. He emphasizes the importance of moving beyond punitive measures to embrace the principles of restorative justice, which seek to heal and rebuild relationships.

- 2 Corinthians 2:6-7: "The punishment inflicted on him by the majority is sufficient. Now instead, you ought to forgive and comfort him, so that he will not be overwhelmed by excessive sorrow."

Principles of Restorative Justice

Forgiveness

Forgiveness is a foundational principle of restorative justice. It involves releasing the offender from the burden of guilt and extending grace, much as God has extended grace to believers through Christ.

- 2 Corinthians 2:7: "Now instead, you ought to forgive and comfort him, so that he will not be overwhelmed by excessive sorrow."

Paul urges the Corinthians to forgive the offender, emphasizing that continued punishment or exclusion could lead to despair and further harm. Forgiveness is essential for the offender's healing and for the restoration of relationships within the community.

Comfort

Alongside forgiveness, Paul emphasizes the need to comfort the repentant offender. Comforting involves providing emotional and spiritual support, helping the individual to overcome guilt and shame, and encouraging their reintegration into the community.

- 2 Corinthians 2:8: "I urge you, therefore, to reaffirm your love for him."

By reaffirming their love and offering comfort, the church can help the offender to heal and to feel valued and accepted once again. This support is crucial for rebuilding trust and fostering a sense of belonging.

Restoration

Restoration is the ultimate goal of restorative justice. It involves not only forgiving and comforting the offender but also actively working to reintegrate them into the community and restore their relationships.

- 2 Corinthians 2:10: "Anyone you forgive, I also forgive. And what I have forgiven—if there was anything to forgive—I have forgiven in the sight of Christ for your sake, in order that Satan might not outwit us. For we are not unaware of his schemes."

Paul's commitment to forgiveness and restoration reflects his understanding of the broader spiritual battle. By restoring the offender, the church can thwart the schemes of Satan, who seeks to sow discord and division.

Practical Steps for Reconciliation

Embracing Repentance

The first step in the process of reconciliation is to embrace the offender's repentance. Genuine repentance involves a recognition of wrongdoing, a heartfelt apology, and a commitment to change.

- 2 Corinthians 7:9-10: "Yet now I am happy, not because you were made sorry, but because your sorrow led you to repentance. For you became sorrowful as God intended and so were not harmed in any way by us. Godly sorrow brings repentance that leads to salvation and leaves no regret, but worldly sorrow brings death."

Paul distinguishes between godly sorrow, which leads to true repentance and transformation, and worldly sorrow, which leads to despair. Embracing repentance means recognizing the offender's genuine contrition and willingness to change.

Offering Forgiveness

Once repentance is acknowledged, the church must offer forgiveness. This involves letting go of resentment and extending grace, following the example of Christ.

- Ephesians 4:32: "Be kind and compassionate to one another, forgiving each other, just as in Christ God forgave you."

Forgiveness is a powerful act of grace that frees both the offender and the community from the burdens of guilt and bitterness.

Providing Comfort and Support

After forgiving the offender, the church should provide comfort and support to help them reintegrate into the community. This involves offering emotional and spiritual support, as well as practical assistance if needed.

- Galatians 6:1-2: "Brothers and sisters, if someone is caught in a sin, you who live by the Spirit should restore that person gently. But watch yourselves, or you also may be tempted. Carry each other's burdens, and in this way you will fulfill the law of Christ."

Providing comfort and support is essential for the offender's healing and for rebuilding trust within the community.

Reaffirming Love

Reaffirming love is a crucial step in the process of reconciliation. It involves actively demonstrating love and acceptance, showing the offender that they are valued and welcomed back into the community.

- 1 Peter 4:8: "Above all, love each other deeply, because love covers over a multitude of sins."

By reaffirming their love, the church can help the offender to feel secure and supported, fostering a sense of belonging and community.

Restoring Relationships

The final step in the process of reconciliation is the restoration of relationships. This involves rebuilding trust, fostering healthy communication, and working towards a harmonious and united community.

- Colossians 3:13-14: "Bear with each other and forgive one another if any of you has a grievance against someone. Forgive as the Lord forgave you. And over all these virtues put on love, which binds them all together in perfect unity."

Restoring relationships requires ongoing effort and commitment from both the offender and the community, but it is essential for achieving true reconciliation and unity.

The Broader Implications for the Church

Preventing Division

By embracing the principles of restorative justice, the church can prevent division and discord. Forgiveness, comfort, and restoration foster a culture of unity and mutual support, helping to maintain the integrity and witness of the church.

Demonstrating the Gospel

The process of reconciliation within the church demonstrates the transformative power of the gospel. By following Christ's example of grace and forgiveness, the church can bear witness to the love and redemption that are central to the Christian faith.

Encouraging Spiritual Growth

The process of reconciliation encourages spiritual growth for both the offender and the community. It challenges individuals to practice forgiveness, compassion, and humility, fostering a deeper relationship with God and with one another.

In 2 Corinthians 2:5-11, Paul emphasizes the importance of forgiving and comforting a repentant offender, reaffirming the church's love for him. His instructions reflect the principles of restorative justice, highlighting the need for forgiveness, comfort, and restoration.

Understanding Paul's guidance on the reconciliation of an offender provides valuable insights for contemporary faith communities. By embracing these principles, churches today can create environments where repentance is encouraged, forgiveness is extended, and relationships are restored.

In the following chapters, we will continue to explore Paul's teachings on restorative justice in 1st and 2nd Corinthians, examining how his instructions can be applied to address various issues within the church and promote a culture of reconciliation and healing. Through this exploration, we aim to provide a comprehensive understanding of restorative justice as a vital aspect of Christian faith and practice.

THE MINISTRY OF RECONCILIATION (2 CORINTHIANS 5:11-21)

In 2 Corinthians 5:11-21, Paul outlines the ministry of reconciliation, describing how God reconciled the world to

Himself through Christ and entrusted this ministry to believers. This profound passage is foundational for understanding restorative justice from a Christian perspective. Paul's teachings highlight the transformative power of reconciliation and the responsibility of believers to carry out this ministry in their lives and communities.

Understanding Reconciliation

God's Initiative in Reconciliation

Reconciliation is the process by which God restores the broken relationship between Himself and humanity through Jesus Christ. Paul emphasizes that this reconciliation is entirely initiated by God, who reaches out to a fallen world with love and grace.

- 2 Corinthians 5:18: "All this is from God, who reconciled us to himself through Christ and gave us the ministry of reconciliation."

God's initiative in reconciliation demonstrates His profound love and desire for restored relationships. It is an act of divine grace that seeks to heal the rift caused by sin and to bring humanity back into communion with Him.

The Role of Christ

Christ plays a central role in the ministry of reconciliation. Through His life, death, and resurrection, Jesus bridges the gap between God and humanity, making it possible for people to be reconciled to God.

- 2 Corinthians 5:19: "That God was reconciling the world to himself in Christ, not counting people's sins against them. And he has committed to us the message of reconciliation."

Christ's sacrificial love and atoning death are the means by which reconciliation is achieved. His resurrection affirms the victory over sin and death, offering new life and restored relationships to all who believe.

The Ministry of Reconciliation Entrusted to Believers

Ambassadors for Christ

Paul describes believers as ambassadors for Christ, entrusted with the message and ministry of reconciliation. This role involves representing Christ to the world and actively participating in the work of reconciliation.

- 2 Corinthians 5:20: "We are therefore Christ's ambassadors, as though God were making his appeal through us. We implore you on Christ's behalf: Be reconciled to God."

As ambassadors, believers are called to live out the principles of reconciliation in their relationships, communities, and broader society. This involves advocating for peace, justice, and restored relationships, reflecting the character and mission of Christ.

The Message of Reconciliation

The message of reconciliation is the good news that through Christ, people can be reconciled to God. This message is central to the Christian faith and mission, calling individuals to repentance, faith, and restored relationships with God and others.

- 2 Corinthians 5:21: "God made him who had no sin to be sin for us so that in him we might become the righteousness of God."

This message emphasizes the transformative power of God's grace, which not only forgives sins but also imparts righteousness and new life. It is a call to experience and extend God's reconciliation in all aspects of life.

Principles of Restorative Justice in the Ministry of Reconciliation

Healing and Restoration

The ministry of reconciliation is fundamentally about healing and restoration. It seeks to repair broken relationships and restore individuals and communities to wholeness.

- Colossians 1:20: "And through him to reconcile to himself all things, whether things on earth or things in heaven, by making peace through his blood, shed on the cross."

This principle is central to restorative justice, which prioritizes repairing harm and restoring relationships over mere punishment or retribution.

Forgiveness and Grace

Forgiveness is a crucial aspect of the ministry of reconciliation. Just as God forgives sins through Christ, believers are called to extend forgiveness to others, promoting healing and restoring relationships.

- Ephesians 4:32: "Be kind and compassionate to one another, forgiving each other, just as in Christ God forgave you."

Extending forgiveness reflects God's grace and enables the process of reconciliation to take place, breaking the cycle of resentment and retaliation.

Justice and Peace

The Ministry of reconciliation also involves seeking justice and peace. This includes addressing systemic injustices, advocating for the oppressed, and working towards a society that reflects God's righteousness and peace.

- Isaiah 61:1: "The Spirit of the Sovereign LORD is on me, because the LORD has anointed me to proclaim good news to the poor. He has sent me to bind up the brokenhearted, to proclaim freedom for the captives and release from darkness for the prisoners."

Justice and peace are integral to restorative justice, which seeks to create conditions where all individuals can flourish and live in harmony.

Practical Steps for Engaging in the Ministry of Reconciliation

Personal Reflection and Repentance

Engaging in the ministry of reconciliation begins with personal reflection and repentance. Believers must examine their own lives, seeking to identify and address areas of brokenness and sin.

- Psalm 139:23-24: "Search me, God, and know my heart; test me and know my anxious thoughts. See if there is any offensive way in me, and lead me in the way everlasting."

Personal reflection and repentance are foundational for experiencing God's reconciliation and extending it to others.

Building Restorative Relationships

Believers are called to build restorative relationships characterized by forgiveness, grace, and mutual support. This involves actively seeking to repair broken relationships and to foster a culture of reconciliation within the community.

- Romans 12:18: "If it is possible, as far as it depends on you, live at peace with everyone."

Building restorative relationships requires intentional effort and a commitment to living out the principles of reconciliation in daily life.

Advocating for Justice and Peace

Engaging in the ministry of reconciliation also involves advocating for justice and peace in broader society. This includes addressing systemic injustices, supporting initiatives that promote peace, and standing in solidarity with the marginalized and oppressed.

- Micah 6:8: "He has shown you, O mortal, what is good. And what does the LORD require of you? To act justly and to love mercy and to walk humbly with your God."

Advocating for justice and peace is a vital aspect of the ministry of reconciliation, reflecting God's heart for a just and harmonious world.

The Broader Implications for the Church

A Witness to the World

The ministry of reconciliation is a powerful witness to the world. As believers live out the principles of reconciliation and restorative justice, they demonstrate the transformative power of the gospel and God's love for all people.

- John 13:35: "By this everyone will know that you are my disciples, if you love one another."

The church's commitment to reconciliation and restorative justice serves as a compelling testimony to the world of the reality of God's kingdom.

Fostering Unity and Community

Engaging in the ministry of reconciliation fosters unity and community within the church. It encourages believers to support one another, to address conflicts constructively, and to work together towards common goals.

- Ephesians 4:3: "Make every effort to keep the unity of the Spirit through the bond of peace."

Unity and community are strengthened as the church embraces its role in the ministry of reconciliation, creating an environment where relationships can thrive.

Encouraging Spiritual Growth

The ministry of reconciliation encourages spiritual growth by challenging believers to live out their faith in practical ways. It fosters a deeper understanding of God's grace and justice, and it encourages believers to grow in their relationship with God and with one another.

- 2 Peter 3:18: "But grow in the grace and knowledge of our Lord and Savior Jesus Christ. To him be glory both now and forever! Amen."

Spiritual growth is nurtured as believers engage in the ministry of reconciliation, deepening their faith and their commitment to God's mission.

In 2 Corinthians 5:11-21, Paul outlines the ministry of reconciliation, describing how God reconciled the world to Himself through Christ and entrusted this ministry to believers. This passage is foundational for understanding restorative justice from a Christian perspective. By embracing the principles of healing, forgiveness, justice, and peace, believers can actively participate in the ministry of reconciliation, reflecting God's love and grace in their lives and communities.

Understanding Paul's teachings on the ministry of reconciliation provides valuable insights for contemporary faith communities. By engaging in this ministry, churches today can create environments where reconciliation and restorative justice thrive, fostering unity, community, and spiritual growth.

In the following chapters, we will continue to explore Paul's teachings on restorative justice in 1st and 2nd Corinthians, examining how his instructions can be applied to address various issues within the church and promote a culture of reconciliation and healing. Through this exploration, we aim to provide a comprehensive

understanding of restorative justice as a vital aspect of Christian faith and practice.

CHAPTER 05

PRACTICAL APPLICATIONS OF RESTORATIVE JUSTICE

Restorative Practices in Church Discipline

Drawing from Paul's teachings, this chapter explores practical ways churches can implement restorative justice in their disciplinary processes. Emphasis is placed on forgiveness, restoration, and the reintegration of offenders. By applying these principles, churches can create a culture that reflects the heart of the gospel and fosters healing and reconciliation within the community.

Understanding Church Discipline

Biblical Basis for Discipline

Church discipline is rooted in biblical teachings that emphasize the need to address sin and maintain the moral integrity of the community. Paul's letters to the Corinthians provide a framework for understanding and implementing discipline in a way that aligns with restorative justice.

- 1 Corinthians 5:12-13: "What business is it of mine to judge those outside the church? Are you not to judge those inside? God will judge those outside. 'Expel the wicked person from among you.'"

- 2 Corinthians 2:6-8: "The punishment inflicted on him by the majority is sufficient. Now instead, you ought to forgive and comfort him, so that he will not be overwhelmed by excessive sorrow. I urge you, therefore, to reaffirm your love for him."

These passages highlight the need for both addressing wrongdoing and seeking the offender's restoration.

Goals of Church Discipline

The primary goals of church discipline are to protect the community, restore the offender, and uphold the church's witness. Restorative justice principles guide these goals by emphasizing healing, reconciliation, and the reintegration of offenders.

1. Protecting the Community: Discipline serves to protect the church from the corrosive effects of sin and to maintain its moral and spiritual integrity.

2. Restoring the Offender: Discipline aims to bring the offender to repentance and to facilitate their healing and restoration.

3. Upholding the Church's Witness: Discipline reflects the church's commitment to holiness and its role as a witness to the transformative power of the gospel.

Implementing Restorative Practices in Church Discipline

Emphasizing Forgiveness

Forgiveness is a foundational principle of restorative justice and is essential in the context of church discipline. Forgiveness involves releasing the offender from the burden of guilt and extending grace, reflecting the forgiveness believers receive from God.

- Matthew 6:14-15: "For if you forgive other people when they sin against you, your heavenly Father will also forgive you. But if you do not forgive others their sins, your Father will not forgive your sins."

Forgiveness should be emphasized throughout the disciplinary process, ensuring that the church community approaches the offender with a spirit of grace and compassion.

Steps for Practicing Forgiveness

1. Acknowledge the Offense: Recognize and name the wrongdoing, ensuring that it is addressed openly and honestly.

2. Seek Repentance: Encourage the offender to acknowledge their sin and to seek forgiveness from God and the community.

3. Extend Grace: Offer forgiveness, releasing the offender from guilt and demonstrating the grace of God.

4. Encourage Reconciliation: Facilitate steps towards repairing relationships and restoring the offender to the community.

Facilitating Restoration

Restoration involves helping the offender to heal and to reintegrate into the church community. This process requires a commitment to the offender's well-being and an emphasis on rehabilitation rather than punishment.

- Galatians 6:1: "Brothers and sisters, if someone is caught in a sin, you who live by the Spirit should restore that person gently. But watch yourselves, or you also may be tempted."

Restoration should be approached gently and with a focus on supporting the offender's spiritual and emotional healing.

Steps for Facilitating Restoration

1. Provide Support: Offer counseling, mentorship, and spiritual guidance to help the offender in their journey of repentance and healing.

2. Encourage Accountability: Establish structures for accountability, ensuring that the offender is supported and guided in their efforts to change.

3. Promote Reconciliation: Facilitate opportunities for the offender to make amends and to rebuild relationships within the community.

4. Celebrate Progress: Acknowledge and celebrate milestones in the offender's journey of restoration, reinforcing their efforts and progress.

Reintegration of Offenders

Reintegration involves welcoming the offender back into the church community and helping them to find their place within it. This process is essential for ensuring that the offender feels valued and accepted, fostering a sense of belonging and purpose.

- 2 Corinthians 2:8: "I urge you, therefore, to reaffirm your love for him."

Reaffirming love and support is crucial for successful reintegration, helping the offender to feel embraced by the community.

Steps for Reintegration

1. Reaffirm Love and Acceptance: Communicate the church's love and acceptance of the offender, ensuring that they feel welcomed and valued.

2. Involve in Community Life: Encourage the offender to participate in church activities and ministries, helping them to rebuild their sense of belonging.

3. Monitor Progress: Continue to monitor the offender's progress, providing ongoing support and guidance as needed.

4. Promote Inclusion: Foster an inclusive environment where the offender can build new relationships and contribute to the life of the church.

Creating a Culture of Restorative Justice

Educating the Congregation

Creating a culture of restorative justice requires educating the congregation about the principles and practices of restorative justice. This education can be provided through sermons, Bible studies, and workshops that teach the biblical foundations of forgiveness, restoration, and reconciliation.

- Ephesians 4:12-13: "To equip his people for works of service, so that the body of Christ may be built up until we all reach unity in the faith and in the knowledge of the Son of God and become mature, attaining to the whole measure of the fullness of Christ."

Education helps to equip the congregation to practice restorative justice in their own lives and to support the church's disciplinary processes.

Modeling Restorative Practices

Church leaders should model restorative practices in their interactions and decision-making processes. By demonstrating forgiveness, compassion, and a commitment to restoration, leaders can set an example for the congregation to follow.

- 1 Peter 5:3: "Not lording it over those entrusted to you, but being examples to the flock."

Modeling restorative practices helps to create a culture where these principles are valued and practiced by all members of the community.

Providing Resources and Support

Providing resources and support is essential for implementing restorative practices in church discipline. This can include offering counseling services, establishing support groups, and providing training for those involved in the disciplinary process.

- Galatians 6:2: "Carry each other's burdens, and in this way you will fulfill the law of Christ."

By providing resources and support, the church can ensure that the disciplinary process is conducted with compassion and effectiveness.

The Broader Implications for the Church

Enhancing Unity and Community

Implementing restorative justice in church discipline enhances unity and community by promoting healing and reconciliation. It helps to build a stronger, more cohesive church that reflects the love and grace of Christ.

- Colossians 3:14: "And over all these virtues put on love, which binds them all together in perfect unity."

A culture of restorative justice fosters a sense of unity and mutual support, strengthening the church's witness to the world.

Demonstrating the Gospel

Restorative justice in church discipline demonstrates the transformative power of the gospel. It shows that the church is a place of grace, forgiveness, and restoration, where individuals can experience the redemptive love of Christ.

- John 13:34-35: "A new command I give you: Love one another. As I have loved you, so you must love one another. By this everyone will know that you are my disciples, if you love one another."

The church's commitment to restorative justice serves as a powerful testimony to the reality of God's kingdom and the transformative power of the gospel.

Encouraging Spiritual Growth

Engaging in restorative justice encourages spiritual growth for both the offender and the community. It challenges individuals to practice forgiveness, compassion, and humility, fostering a deeper relationship with God and with one another.

- James 5:16: "Therefore confess your sins to each other and pray for each other so that you may be healed. The prayer of a righteous person is powerful and effective."

Spiritual growth is nurtured as believers engage in the process of restoration and reconciliation, deepening their faith and their commitment to God's mission.

Implementing restorative justice in church discipline involves emphasizing forgiveness, facilitating restoration, and reintegrating offenders into the community. By applying these principles, churches can create a culture that reflects the heart of the gospel and fosters healing and reconciliation within the community.

Understanding and practicing restorative justice in church discipline provides valuable insights for contemporary faith communities. By embracing these principles, churches today can create environments where sin is confronted constructively, relationships are restored, and the community's witness is strengthened.

In the following chapters, we will continue to explore Paul's teachings on restorative justice in 1st and 2nd Corinthians, examining how his instructions can be applied to address various issues within the church and promote a culture of reconciliation and healing. Through this exploration, we aim to provide a comprehensive understanding of restorative justice as a vital aspect of Christian faith and practice.

RESTORATIVE JUSTICE IN COMMUNITY LIFE

Restorative justice principles extend beyond formal disciplinary actions and can be applied to various aspects of community life. This chapter explores how these principles can be integrated into everyday interactions within the church, including conflict resolution, support for victims, and fostering a culture of reconciliation. By embracing restorative justice, churches can create a nurturing environment that reflects the love and grace of Christ.

Conflict Resolution

Biblical Foundation for Resolving Conflicts

The Bible provides clear guidance on resolving conflicts within the Christian community. Jesus and the apostles emphasized the importance of reconciliation and peaceful relationships.

- Matthew 18:15-17: "If your brother or sister sins, go and point out their fault, just between the two of you. If they listen to you, you have won them over. But if they will not listen, take one or two others along, so that 'every matter may be established by the testimony of two or three witnesses.' If they still refuse to listen, tell it to the church; and if they refuse to listen even to the church, treat them as you would a pagan or a tax collector."

- Romans 12:18: "If it is possible, as far as it depends on you, live at peace with everyone."

These passages emphasize direct, personal efforts to resolve conflicts, involving the community only when necessary, and always seeking reconciliation.

Steps for Conflict Resolution

1. Direct Communication: Encourage individuals to address conflicts directly with the person involved, fostering open and honest communication.

2. Mediation: If direct communication fails, involve a neutral third party to mediate the dispute and facilitate understanding.

3. Community Involvement: As a last resort, bring the conflict before the church community for resolution, ensuring that the process is guided by love and a commitment to reconciliation.

4. Follow-Up: Monitor the situation after resolution to ensure that relationships are healed and that the conflict does not resurface.

Tools for Conflict Resolution

- Active Listening: Teach and practice active listening skills, ensuring that all parties feel heard and understood.

- Empathy: Encourage empathy, helping individuals to understand each other's perspectives and to find common ground.

- Conflict Resolution Training: Provide training for church leaders and members on conflict resolution techniques and biblical principles.

Support for Victims

Recognizing the Needs of Victims

Supporting victims is a crucial aspect of restorative justice. The church must recognize the needs of victims and provide appropriate care and support.

- Isaiah 61:1: "The Spirit of the Sovereign LORD is on me, because the LORD has anointed me to proclaim good news to the poor. He has sent me to bind up the brokenhearted, to proclaim freedom for the captives and release from darkness for the prisoners."

Victims often need emotional, spiritual, and sometimes physical support to heal from their experiences.

Practical Steps for Supporting Victims

1. Creating Safe Spaces: Establish safe and confidential environments where victims can share their stories and seek support.

2. Providing Counseling: Offer professional counseling services to help victims process their experiences and begin the healing journey.

3. Offering Spiritual Support: Provide spiritual support through prayer, pastoral care, and scripture, helping victims find comfort and hope in their faith.

4. Ensuring Justice: Advocate for justice on behalf of victims, addressing the harm they have experienced and working to prevent future harm.

Resources for Victim Support

- Support Groups: Establish support groups where victims can connect with others who have experienced similar situations, providing mutual support and encouragement.

- Resource Lists: Compile and distribute lists of local resources, including counseling centers, support organizations, and legal aid.

- Training for Church Leaders: Train church leaders to recognize and respond to the needs of victims, ensuring that they are equipped to provide effective support.

Fostering a Culture of Reconciliation

Building a Foundation of Trust

Fostering a culture of reconciliation requires building a foundation of trust within the church community. Trust is established through consistent actions that reflect integrity, honesty, and care.

- Proverbs 3:3-4: "Let love and faithfulness never leave you; bind them around your neck, write them on the tablet of your heart. Then you will win favor and a good name in the sight of God and man."

By cultivating an environment where trust is valued and upheld, the church can create a safe space for reconciliation to occur.

Promoting Open Communication

Open communication is essential for reconciliation. Encourage transparency and honesty in all interactions, creating an environment where members feel comfortable expressing their thoughts and concerns.

- Ephesians 4:25: "Therefore each of you must put off falsehood and speak truthfully to your neighbor, for we are all members of one body."

Open communication fosters understanding and prevents misunderstandings, making it easier to address conflicts and promote reconciliation.

Encouraging Forgiveness and Grace

Forgiveness and grace are central to a culture of reconciliation. Teach and model these principles, encouraging members to forgive one another and to extend grace in all situations.

- Colossians 3:13: "Bear with each other and forgive one another if any of you has a grievance against someone. Forgive as the Lord forgave you."

Forgiveness and grace pave the way for healing and restored relationships, helping to create a community that reflects the love of Christ.

Celebrating Reconciliation

Celebrate moments of reconciliation within the church, highlighting stories of forgiveness, healing, and restored relationships. This not only encourages those involved but also inspires the entire community to embrace the principles of restorative justice.

- Luke 15:10: "In the same way, I tell you, there is rejoicing in the presence of the angels of God over one sinner who repents."

By celebrating reconciliation, the church reinforces the importance of these principles and fosters a culture where they are valued and practiced.

Practical Applications in Everyday Community Life

Everyday Interactions

Integrate restorative justice principles into everyday interactions within the church community. Encourage members to practice active listening, empathy, and forgiveness in their daily lives, fostering a culture of mutual respect and care.

- Philippians 2:3-4: "Do nothing out of selfish ambition or vain conceit. Rather, in humility value others above yourselves, not looking to your own interests but each of you to the interests of the others."

By applying these principles in everyday interactions, the church can create a cohesive and supportive community.

Church Programs and Activities

Incorporate restorative justice principles into church programs and activities. This includes youth groups, small groups, outreach programs, and other church ministries, ensuring that all aspects of church life reflect the values of reconciliation and restorative justice.

- Acts 2:44-47: "All the believers were together and had everything in common. They sold property and possessions to give to anyone who had need. Every day they continued to meet together in the temple courts. They broke bread in their homes and ate together with glad and sincere hearts, praising God and enjoying the favor of all the people. And the Lord added to their number daily those who were being saved."

By integrating restorative justice into all areas of church life, the community can consistently reflect the heart of the gospel.

Training and Education

Provide ongoing training and education on restorative justice principles for church members. This can include workshops, seminars, and Bible studies that teach the biblical foundations and practical applications of restorative justice.

- 2 Timothy 2:15: "Do your best to present yourself to God as one approved, a worker who does not need to be ashamed and who correctly handles the word of truth."

Education equips members to live out these principles effectively, fostering a community that is knowledgeable and committed to restorative justice.

The Broader Implications for the Church

Strengthening Community Bonds

Implementing restorative justice in community life strengthens the bonds between church members. It fosters a sense of unity, mutual support, and shared purpose, helping to create a strong and resilient community.

- 1 Corinthians 12:12-13: "Just as a body, though one, has many parts, but all its many parts form one body, so it is with Christ. For we were all baptized by one Spirit so as to form one body—whether Jews or Gentiles, slave or free—and we were all given the one Spirit to drink."

Strong community bonds enhance the church's ability to support one another and to navigate challenges together.

Enhancing the Church's Witness

A church that embodies restorative justice principles serves as a powerful witness to the world. It demonstrates the transformative power of the gospel and reflects the love and grace of Christ to those outside the church.

- John 13:34-35: "A new command I give you: Love one another. As I have loved you, so you must love one another. By this everyone will know that you are my disciples, if you love one another."

The church's commitment to restorative justice enhances its witness and attracts others to the message of Christ.

Encouraging Spiritual Growth

Engaging in restorative justice encourages spiritual growth for all members. It challenges individuals to practice forgiveness, empathy, and humility, fostering a deeper relationship with God and with one another.

- Hebrews 10:24-25: "And let us consider how we may spur one another on toward love and good deeds, not giving up meeting together, as some are in the habit of doing, but encouraging one another—and all the more as you see the Day approaching."

Spiritual growth is nurtured as members engage in the practices of restorative justice, deepening their faith and their commitment to God's mission.

Restorative justice principles can be applied to various aspects of community life, including conflict resolution, support for victims, and fostering a culture of reconciliation. By integrating these

CHAPTER 06

CHALLENGES AND OPPORTUNITIES

Addressing Misunderstandings

Restorative justice is often misunderstood or misapplied. This chapter addresses common misconceptions and provides clarity on the true nature and goals of restorative justice. By addressing these misunderstandings, we can better appreciate the transformative power of restorative justice and harness its full potential within the church and broader community.

Common Misconceptions About Restorative Justice

Misconception 1: Restorative Justice is Soft on Crime

One of the most prevalent misconceptions about restorative justice is that it is soft on crime or wrongdoing. Critics argue that restorative justice emphasizes forgiveness and reconciliation at the expense of accountability and justice.

- Clarification: Restorative justice is not about excusing or minimizing wrongdoing. It involves holding offenders accountable for their actions and encouraging them to take responsibility for the harm they have caused. The goal is to repair the damage, restore relationships, and prevent future harm. Accountability is a key component of restorative justice, ensuring that offenders understand the impact of their actions and take meaningful steps toward making amends.

Misconception 2: Restorative Justice Neglects the Needs of Victims

Another common misconception is that restorative justice prioritizes the needs of offenders over those of victims. Some believe that focusing on the rehabilitation and reintegration of offenders can overshadow the harm suffered by victims and their need for justice.

- Clarification: Restorative justice places a strong emphasis on the needs and healing of victims. It seeks to address the harm caused by wrongdoing and to provide victims with an opportunity to express their feelings, receive support, and be involved in the resolution process. Restorative justice aims to empower victims, ensuring that their voices are heard and their needs are met. It recognizes that true justice involves healing for all parties affected by wrongdoing.

Misconception 3: Restorative Justice is Only Suitable for Minor Offenses

Some people believe that restorative justice is only appropriate for minor offenses or non-violent crimes. This misconception limits the application of restorative justice to less serious situations, overlooking its potential to address more significant and complex cases.

- Clarification: Restorative justice can be applied to a wide range of offenses, including serious and violent crimes. Its principles of accountability, healing, and reconciliation are relevant in various contexts. While the process may differ depending on the severity of the offense, restorative justice has been successfully used in cases of serious crimes, providing meaningful resolutions that traditional justice systems often fail to achieve.

Misconception 4: Restorative Justice is Incompatible with Traditional Justice Systems

Another misconception is that restorative justice cannot coexist with traditional justice systems. Some argue that restorative justice is too lenient and conflicts with the punitive nature of conventional justice approaches.

- Clarification: Restorative justice can complement traditional justice systems. It offers an alternative or additional pathway for resolving conflicts and addressing harm. In some cases, restorative justice processes are integrated within traditional justice systems, providing a holistic approach that incorporates accountability, healing, and restoration. Both systems can work together to ensure that justice is served in a way that promotes long-term healing and reconciliation.

Clarifying the True Nature and Goals of Restorative Justice

Principle 1: Accountability and Responsibility

Restorative justice emphasizes accountability and responsibility. Offenders are encouraged to acknowledge their actions, understand the impact of their behavior, and take responsibility for repairing the harm.

- Scriptural Basis: Ezekiel 18:30: "Therefore, you Israelites, I will judge each of you according to your own ways, declares the Sovereign LORD. Repent! Turn away from all your offenses; then sin will not be your downfall."

Accountability involves recognizing wrongdoing, making amends, and committing to positive change.

Principle 2: Healing and Restoration

The primary goal of restorative justice is healing and restoration. It seeks to repair the damage caused by wrongdoing and to restore relationships between the victim, the offender, and the community.

- Scriptural Basis: Isaiah 61:1: "The Spirit of the Sovereign LORD is on me, because the LORD has anointed me to proclaim good news to the poor. He has sent me to bind up the brokenhearted, to proclaim freedom for the captives and release from darkness for the prisoners."

Healing and restoration involve addressing the needs of all parties, fostering reconciliation, and promoting long-term well-being.

Principle 3: Inclusion and Participation

Restorative justice involves the inclusion and participation of all stakeholders in the resolution process. This includes victims, offenders, and community members, who work together to find a constructive and meaningful resolution.

- Scriptural Basis: Matthew 18:20: "For where two or three gather in my name, there am I with them."

Inclusion and participation ensure that all voices are heard, and that the resolution process is collaborative and holistic.

Principle 4: Prevention and Transformation

Restorative justice aims to prevent future harm and to transform individuals and communities. By addressing the root causes of wrongdoing and fostering positive change, restorative justice promotes long-term healing and resilience.

- Scriptural Basis: Romans 12:2: "Do not conform to the pattern of this world, but be transformed by the renewing of your mind. Then you will be able to test and approve what God's will is—his good, pleasing and perfect will."

Prevention and transformation involve creating supportive environments that encourage personal growth, community cohesion, and sustainable peace.

Addressing Challenges in Implementing Restorative Justice

Challenge 1: Resistance to Change

Implementing restorative justice can encounter resistance from individuals and institutions accustomed to traditional punitive approaches. Overcoming this resistance requires education, advocacy, and demonstrating the effectiveness of restorative justice.

Strategies for Overcoming Resistance

1. Education and Awareness: Provide education and awareness programs that highlight the principles and benefits of restorative justice. Use workshops, seminars, and real-life examples to demonstrate its effectiveness.

2. Engage Stakeholders: Involve key stakeholders, including church leaders, community members, and justice system representatives, in the conversation. Their support and endorsement can help to build acceptance and momentum.

3. Pilot Programs: Implement pilot programs to showcase the positive outcomes of restorative justice. Use these programs as evidence to build support and expand its application.

Challenge 2: Ensuring Adequate Resources and Training

Successful implementation of restorative justice requires adequate resources and training. This includes trained facilitators, counseling services, and support structures for victims and offenders.

Strategies for Ensuring Resources and Training

1. Invest in Training: Provide comprehensive training for facilitators, church leaders, and community members involved in restorative justice processes. Ensure they have the skills and knowledge to conduct these processes effectively.

2. Collaborate with Experts: Partner with organizations and experts in restorative justice to access resources, training, and support. Collaboration can enhance the quality and reach of restorative justice initiatives.

3. Allocate Resources: Allocate sufficient resources, including funding and personnel, to support restorative justice programs. Ensure that these programs are sustainable and well-resourced.

Challenge 3: Balancing Justice and Compassion

Balancing justice and compassion can be challenging, especially in cases involving serious offenses. It is essential to ensure that restorative justice processes are fair, transparent, and uphold the principles of accountability and healing.

Strategies for Balancing Justice and Compassion

1. Establish Clear Guidelines: Develop clear guidelines and protocols for restorative justice processes. Ensure that these guidelines emphasize both accountability and compassion.

2. Maintain Transparency: Ensure transparency in all restorative justice processes. Keep all parties informed and involved, and maintain open communication throughout.

3. Uphold Fairness: Uphold fairness in decision-making and resolution processes. Ensure that the needs and perspectives of all parties are considered and respected.

Opportunities for Advancing Restorative Justice

Opportunity 1: Enhancing Community Cohesion

Restorative justice can enhance community cohesion by fostering strong, supportive relationships and promoting a culture of mutual respect and care.

Strategies for Enhancing Community Cohesion

1. Community Building Activities: Organize community building activities that bring people together and

promote understanding and solidarity. These activities can include workshops, social events, and collaborative projects.

2. Foster Inclusivity: Foster an inclusive environment where all community members feel valued and respected. Encourage diversity and inclusivity in all aspects of community life.

3. Promote Mutual Support: Promote mutual support and care within the community. Encourage members to support one another, particularly in times of conflict or crisis.

Opportunity 2: Demonstrating the Transformative Power of the Gospel

Implementing restorative justice provides an opportunity to demonstrate the transformative power of the gospel. It reflects the principles of grace, forgiveness, and reconciliation central to the Christian faith.

Strategies for Demonstrating the Transformative Power of the Gospel

1. Highlight Biblical Principles: Highlight the biblical principles that underpin restorative justice. Use scripture to demonstrate how restorative justice aligns with the teachings of Jesus and the apostles.

2. Share Success Stories: Share success stories and testimonies of individuals and communities transformed by

restorative justice. Use these stories to inspire and encourage others.

3. Incorporate into Ministry: Incorporate restorative justice principles into various aspects of ministry, including preaching, teaching, and pastoral care. Use ministry opportunities to promote and practice restorative justice.

Opportunity 3: Addressing Systemic Injustice

Restorative justice can address systemic injustice by promoting fairness, equity, and healing in broader societal contexts. It provides a framework for addressing root causes of injustice and promoting sustainable change.

Strategies for Addressing Systemic Injustice

1. Advocate for Policy Change: Advocate for policy changes that support restorative justice initiatives and address systemic injustices. Work with policymakers and organizations to promote restorative justice principles.

2. Engage in Social Justice Initiatives

: Engage in social justice initiatives that align with restorative justice principles. Support efforts to address issues such as poverty, discrimination, and inequality.

3. Educate and Raise Awareness: Educate the broader community about restorative justice and its potential to address systemic injustice. Raise awareness through public campaigns, educational programs, and community outreach.

Addressing misunderstandings about restorative justice is essential for harnessing its full potential. By clarifying its true nature and goals, we can better appreciate the transformative power of restorative justice and effectively implement its principles within the church and broader community.

Understanding and addressing common misconceptions provides valuable insights for contemporary faith communities. By embracing restorative justice, churches today can create environments where accountability, healing, and reconciliation thrive, fostering unity and reflecting the love and grace of Christ.

In the following chapters, we will continue to explore Paul's teachings on restorative justice in 1st and 2nd Corinthians, examining how his instructions can be applied to address various issues within the church and promote a culture of reconciliation and healing. Through this exploration, we aim to provide a comprehensive understanding of restorative justice as a vital aspect of Christian faith and practice.

BUILDING A RESTORATIVE CULTURE

Creating a culture that embraces restorative justice requires intentional effort and a commitment to fostering an environment where healing, reconciliation, and restoration are prioritized. This chapter offers practical steps for churches and communities to build such a culture, emphasizing the importance of education, training, and leadership. By embedding restorative justice principles into the fabric of community life, churches can reflect the love and grace of Christ and promote unity and healing.

The Importance of Education

Biblical Foundation for Education

Education is a critical component of building a restorative culture. The Bible underscores the importance of teaching and learning, emphasizing that knowledge and understanding are essential for spiritual growth and community well-being.

- Proverbs 4:7: "The beginning of wisdom is this: Get wisdom. Though it cost all you have, get understanding."

- 2 Timothy 2:15: "Do your best to present yourself to God as one approved, a worker who does not need to be ashamed and who correctly handles the word of truth."

By educating members about restorative justice principles, churches can equip them with the knowledge and skills needed to practice these principles in their daily lives.

Steps for Implementing Education

1. Develop Educational Programs: Create programs that educate members about restorative justice, its biblical foundations, and practical applications. These programs can include sermons, Bible studies, workshops, and seminars.

2. Use Diverse Learning Methods: Employ various learning methods to cater to different learning styles. This can include lectures, group discussions, role-playing, and multimedia resources.

3. Incorporate Restorative Justice into Existing Curricula: Integrate restorative justice principles into existing educational curricula, ensuring that these principles are taught across all age groups and ministry areas.

4. Provide Resources: Offer books, articles, and other resources that members can use to deepen their understanding of restorative justice.

Example: Restorative Justice Workshop

Organize a workshop that covers the basics of restorative justice, including its definition, principles, and biblical foundations. Use real-life examples and case studies to illustrate how restorative justice can be applied in various contexts. Provide opportunities for participants to practice restorative justice techniques through role-playing exercises.

The Role of Training

Importance of Skill Development

Training is essential for developing the skills needed to implement restorative justice effectively. This includes skills such as active listening, mediation, conflict resolution, and facilitation.

- Ephesians 4:12-13: "To equip his people for works of service, so that the body of Christ may be built up until we all reach unity in the faith and in the knowledge of the Son of God and become mature, attaining to the whole measure of the fullness of Christ."

Equipping members with these skills helps to ensure that restorative justice processes are conducted with competence and care.

Steps for Implementing Training

1. Identify Training Needs: Assess the specific training needs of your community, identifying the skills and knowledge gaps that need to be addressed.

2. Develop Training Programs: Create training programs that focus on the essential skills for restorative justice. These programs can include both theoretical and practical components.

3. Use Qualified Trainers: Engage qualified trainers with experience in restorative justice to deliver training sessions. This ensures that participants receive high-quality instruction and guidance.

4. Offer Ongoing Training: Provide ongoing training opportunities to reinforce skills and keep members updated on best practices in restorative justice.

Example: Conflict Resolution Training

Offer a training program focused on conflict resolution skills. The program can include sessions on active listening, empathy, negotiation, and mediation. Use role-playing exercises to give participants hands-on experience in resolving conflicts in a restorative manner.

The Role of Leadership

Leadership as a Model

Effective leadership is crucial for building a restorative culture. Leaders must model restorative justice principles in their actions and decision-making, demonstrating a commitment to accountability, healing, and reconciliation.

- 1 Peter 5:2-3: "Be shepherds of God's flock that is under your care, watching over them—not because you must, but because you are willing, as God wants you to be; not pursuing dishonest gain, but eager to serve; not lording it over those entrusted to you, but being examples to the flock."

By exemplifying restorative justice, leaders can inspire and guide the community in embracing these principles.

Steps for Leadership Development

1. Provide Leadership Training: Offer training programs for church leaders that focus on restorative justice principles and leadership skills. Ensure that leaders are equipped to model and promote these principles.

2. Foster Accountability: Create structures for accountability among leaders, ensuring that they uphold restorative justice principles in their actions and decisions.

3. Encourage Collaborative Leadership: Promote a collaborative leadership style that values input and participation from all members of the community. This fosters a sense of ownership and shared responsibility for building a restorative culture.

4. Recognize and Reward Restorative Practices: Acknowledge and celebrate leaders who exemplify restorative justice in their work. This reinforces the importance of these principles and encourages others to follow their example.

Example: Leadership Retreat

Organize a retreat for church leaders focused on restorative justice. Include sessions on the biblical foundations of restorative justice, practical applications in leadership, and strategies for modeling restorative practices. Provide opportunities for leaders to reflect on their own practices and to develop action plans for promoting restorative justice in their areas of responsibility.

Creating Structures and Policies

Establishing Supportive Structures

Creating a restorative culture requires establishing structures and policies that support restorative justice practices. This includes setting up systems for conflict resolution, victim support, and offender reintegration.

- Galatians 6:2: "Carry each other's burdens, and in this way you will fulfill the law of Christ."

Supportive structures ensure that restorative justice principles are embedded into the community's operations and practices.

Steps for Creating Structures

1. Develop Restorative Justice Policies: Create policies that outline the community's commitment to restorative justice and provide guidelines for implementing restorative practices.

2. Establish Restorative Justice Teams: Form teams of trained individuals who can facilitate restorative justice processes, such as mediating conflicts and supporting victims and offenders.

3. Set Up Support Systems: Establish support systems for victims and offenders, including counseling services, support groups, and mentorship programs.

4. Create Monitoring and Evaluation Systems: Implement systems for monitoring and evaluating the effectiveness of restorative justice practices. Use feedback to make continuous improvements.

Example: Restorative Justice Policy

Develop a policy document that outlines the church's commitment to restorative justice. Include sections on the principles of restorative justice, the processes for conflict resolution, the support systems for victims and offenders, and the roles and responsibilities of church members and leaders.

Promoting a Restorative Culture

Encouraging Community Engagement

Promoting a restorative culture involves encouraging community engagement and participation. Create opportunities for members to get involved in restorative justice initiatives and to contribute to the community's efforts to promote healing and reconciliation.

- Hebrews 10:24-25: "And let us consider how we may spur one another on toward love and good deeds, not giving up meeting together, as some are in the habit of doing, but encouraging one another—and all the more as you see the Day approaching."

Engagement fosters a sense of ownership and commitment to building a restorative culture.

Steps for Encouraging Engagement

1. Organize Community Events: Host events that promote restorative justice, such as community forums, service projects, and awareness campaigns.

2. Encourage Volunteering: Provide opportunities for members to volunteer in restorative justice initiatives, such as facilitating support groups or participating in mediation processes.

3. Promote Storytelling: Encourage members to share their experiences with restorative justice, highlighting the positive impact of these practices on their lives and the community.

4. Recognize Contributions: Acknowledge and celebrate the contributions of individuals who actively promote restorative justice. This reinforces the value of their efforts and encourages others to get involved.

Example: Community Forum on Restorative Justice

Host a community forum where members can learn about restorative justice, share their experiences, and discuss how to implement restorative practices in the church. Use the forum to generate ideas, build momentum, and foster a sense of collective responsibility for building a restorative culture.

The Broader Implications for the Church

Strengthening Unity and Community

Building a restorative culture strengthens unity and community within the church. It promotes mutual respect, understanding, and support, helping to create a cohesive and resilient community.

- Colossians 3:14: "And over all these virtues put on love, which binds them all together in perfect unity."

A restorative culture enhances the church's ability to support one another and to navigate challenges together.

Enhancing the Church's Witness

A church that embodies restorative justice principles serves as a powerful witness to the world. It demonstrates the transformative power of the gospel and reflects the love and grace of Christ to those outside the church.

- John 13:34-35: "A new command I give you: Love one another. As I have loved you, so you must love one another. By this everyone will know that you are my disciples, if you love one another."

The church's commitment to restorative justice enhances its witness and attracts others to the message of Christ.

Encouraging Spiritual Growth

Engaging in restorative justice encourages spiritual growth for all members. It challenges individuals to practice forgiveness, empathy, and humility, fostering a deeper relationship with God and with one another.

- James 5:16: "Therefore confess your sins to each other and pray for each other so that you may be healed. The prayer of a righteous person is powerful and effective."

Spiritual growth is nurtured as members engage in the practices of restorative justice, deepening their faith and their commitment to God's mission.

Building a restorative culture requires intentional effort and a commitment to education, training, and leadership. By integrating restorative justice principles into the fabric of community life, churches can reflect the love and grace of Christ and promote unity and healing. Understanding and applying these principles provides valuable insights for contemporary faith communities, helping them to create environments where accountability, healing, and reconciliation thrive.

In the following chapters, we will continue to explore Paul's teachings on restorative justice in 1st and 2nd Corinthians, examining how his instructions can be applied to address various issues within the church and promote a culture of reconciliation and healing. Through this exploration, we aim to provide a comprehensive

understanding of restorative justice as a vital aspect of Christian faith and practice.

CHAPTER 07

GOING FROM 2 CORINTHIANS 5 TO ROMANS 5

In 2 Corinthians 5, Paul outlines the ministry of reconciliation, highlighting how God reconciled the world to Himself through Christ and entrusted this ministry to believers. This passage has profound implications for restorative justice, particularly in how sins no longer have to be "counted against" offending persons (2 Corinthians 5:19). We no longer view offenders from a "worldly point of view," which binds people's identity to their past actions. This chapter explores these ideas in depth, linking them with Paul's teachings in Romans 5 to provide a comprehensive understanding of restorative justice.

The Transformative Power of Reconciliation

Sins No Longer Counted Against Us

In 2 Corinthians 5:19, Paul emphasizes that through Christ, God is no longer counting people's sins against them.

This radical shift underscores the essence of reconciliation and restorative justice.

- 2 Corinthians 5:19: "That God was reconciling the world to himself in Christ, not counting people's sins against them. And he has committed to us the message of reconciliation."

This idea is foundational for restorative justice. It means that past actions do not define a person's identity or future. Instead, there is a focus on healing, restoration, and the potential for transformation.

A New Perspective on Offenders

Paul calls believers to adopt a new perspective, no longer viewing people from a worldly point of view. This means seeing individuals as more than their past mistakes and recognizing their inherent worth and potential for change.

- 2 Corinthians 5:16: "So from now on we regard no one from a worldly point of view. Though we once regarded Christ in this way, we do so no longer."

This perspective is crucial for restorative justice, which seeks to restore relationships and reintegrate individuals into the community.

Linking to Romans 5: The Basis for Reconciliation

In Romans 5, Paul provides a theological foundation for reconciliation, emphasizing the grace and love of God that make restoration possible.

- Romans 5:1-2: "Therefore, since we have been justified through faith, we have peace with God through our Lord Jesus Christ, through whom we have gained access by faith into this grace in which we now stand. And we boast in the hope of the glory of God."

Paul highlights that reconciliation is rooted in God's grace, which justifies and restores us, giving us peace and hope.

Implications for Restorative Justice

Forgiveness and Grace

Both 2 Corinthians 5 and Romans 5 emphasize the themes of forgiveness and grace. These are central to restorative justice, which seeks to offer forgiveness and to extend grace to offenders, allowing them to make amends and rebuild their lives.

- Romans 5:8: "But God demonstrates his own love for us in this: While we were still sinners, Christ died for us."

This verse underscores the unconditional nature of God's love and forgiveness, which should inspire us to extend the same grace to others.

Identity and Transformation

Restorative justice focuses on the potential for transformation, recognizing that individuals are not defined by their past actions but by their capacity for change and growth.

- 2 Corinthians 5:17: "Therefore, if anyone is in Christ, the new creation has come: The old has gone, the new is here!"

This transformative perspective aligns with restorative justice, which seeks to help offenders become new creations, leaving their past behind and embracing a new future.

Reconciliation and Community

Paul's teachings in both 2 Corinthians and Romans highlight the importance of reconciliation and community. Restorative justice seeks to restore relationships and to reintegrate individuals into the community, fostering a sense of belonging and mutual support.

- Romans 5:10-11: "For if, while we were God's enemies, we were reconciled to him through the death of his Son, how much more, having been reconciled, shall we be saved through his life! Not only is this so, but we also boast in God through our Lord Jesus Christ, through whom we have now received reconciliation."

Reconciliation is not just a personal transformation but a communal restoration, reflecting the interconnectedness of the body of Christ.

Practical Steps for Implementing Restorative Justice

Embracing a New Perspective

Churches and communities must embrace the new perspective Paul advocates, viewing individuals not from a worldly point of view but as potential new creations in Christ.

1. Teach and Preach: Regularly teach and preach about the principles of forgiveness, grace, and transformation, helping members to internalize these values.

2. Promote Understanding: Use educational programs to promote understanding of restorative justice and its biblical foundations.

3. Model the Perspective: Leaders should model this perspective in their actions and decisions, demonstrating grace and forgiveness in tangible ways.

Creating Opportunities for Transformation

Provide opportunities for offenders to demonstrate their repentance and to work towards transformation.

1. Support Programs: Establish support programs that provide counseling, mentorship, and resources to help offenders change their behavior and rebuild their lives.

2. Volunteer Opportunities: Create volunteer opportunities where offenders can give back to the community, demonstrating their commitment to making amends.

3. Accountability Structures: Implement accountability structures that support and monitor the offender's progress, ensuring they have the guidance and support they need.

Fostering Reconciliation and Community

Work actively to foster reconciliation and to reintegrate individuals into the community.

1. Reconciliation Processes: Establish processes for reconciliation that involve dialogue, mediation, and mutual agreement on steps for restoration.

2. Community Support: Encourage community support for offenders, helping them to feel welcomed and valued as they reintegrate.

3. Celebrate Restoration: Celebrate stories of restoration and transformation, highlighting the positive outcomes of restorative justice.

Addressing Challenges

Overcoming Resistance

Resistance to restorative justice can come from a desire for retributive justice or a lack of understanding of restorative principles.

1. Education and Advocacy: Educate the community about the benefits of restorative justice and advocate for its principles through real-life examples and testimonies.

2. Dialogue and Discussion: Facilitate open dialogues and discussions where concerns and questions about restorative justice can be addressed.

3. Lead by Example: Leaders should lead by example, demonstrating the effectiveness and importance of restorative justice in their own actions.

Ensuring Balance

Balancing grace with accountability is essential for restorative justice to be effective.

1. Clear Guidelines: Develop clear guidelines that outline the principles and processes of restorative justice, ensuring that both grace and accountability are upheld.

2. Training for Facilitators: Provide training for those who facilitate restorative justice processes, ensuring they are equipped to maintain this balance.

3. Regular Review: Regularly review restorative justice practices to ensure they are being implemented effectively and fairly.

The Broader Implications for the Church

Reflecting Christ's Love

By embracing restorative justice, the church reflects Christ's love and forgiveness, demonstrating the transformative power of the gospel.

- John 13:34-35: "A new command I give you: Love one another. As I have loved you, so you must love one another. By this everyone will know that you are my disciples, if you love one another."

Restorative justice showcases the church as a place of grace, healing, and transformation.

Strengthening Community Bonds

Implementing restorative justice strengthens community bonds, fostering a sense of unity and mutual support.

- Ephesians 4:3: "Make every effort to keep the unity of the Spirit through the bond of peace."

A restorative culture helps to build a resilient and cohesive community.

Enhancing the Church's Witness

A church that practices restorative justice serves as a powerful witness to the world, demonstrating the reconciling work of Christ.

- Matthew 5:14-16: "You are the light of the world. A town built on a hill cannot be hidden. Neither do people light a lamp and put it under a bowl. Instead they put it on its stand, and it gives light to everyone in the house. In the same way, let your light shine before others, that they may see your good deeds and glorify your Father in heaven."

Restorative justice enhances the church's witness, attracting others to the transformative message of the gospel.

The passage in 2 Corinthians 5 provides a profound foundation for restorative justice, emphasizing that sins are no longer counted against offenders and that we should no longer view people from a worldly point of view. Linking this with Romans 5, we see the theological basis for reconciliation rooted in God's grace and love. By embracing these principles, churches can build a restorative culture that promotes healing, reconciliation, and transformation.

Understanding and applying these principles provides valuable insights for contemporary faith communities. By integrating restorative justice into their practices, churches can create environments where accountability, healing, and reconciliation thrive, reflecting the love and grace of Christ in powerful and transformative ways.

In the following chapters, we will continue to explore Paul's teachings on restorative justice, examining how his instructions can be applied to address various issues within the church and promote a culture of reconciliation and healing. Through this exploration, we aim to provide a comprehensive understanding of restorative justice as a vital aspect of Christian faith and practice.

CHAPTER 08

THE RIPPLE EFFECT OF RESTORATIVE JUSTICE

Restorative practitioners speak of the ripple effect caused by harms and crimes, which spread pain and mistrust, creating protectiveness in those most affected and impacting wider circles with negativity. Traditional justice processes that add more pain and mistrust to this negative contagion can exacerbate alienation and heartache. When legal matters diminish the true search for solutions to the harm done, more alienation and heartache can happen. Romans 5:20 highlights the limitations of law in addressing sin, stating, "All that passing laws against sin did was produce more lawbreakers." In contrast, God's future-leaning realm of justice, characterized by "aggressive forgiveness" or grace, offers a transformative approach. This chapter explores the ripple effect of restorative justice and its potential to bring healing and reconciliation.

The Ripple Effect of Harm and Crime

The Spread of Pain and Mistrust

When harm or crime occurs, its effects ripple outwards, impacting not only the direct victims but also their families, friends, and the broader community. This spread of pain and mistrust can create a cycle of protectiveness and further harm.

- Illustration: A theft in a community can lead to the victim feeling violated and fearful, their family members becoming overprotective, and neighbors growing suspicious of each other. The initial harm creates a ripple effect of negativity and distrust.

The Impact on Victims

Victims of harm or crime often experience deep emotional and psychological effects. If their needs are not adequately addressed, they can remain trapped by the weight of the past.

- Example: A victim of assault who does not receive proper support and counseling may struggle with ongoing fear, anxiety, and a sense of vulnerability, affecting their ability to move forward and rebuild their life.

The Limitations of Traditional Justice

Traditional justice systems, which often focus on punishment rather than healing, can add to the ripple effect of harm. By emphasizing retribution over restoration, these systems can leave victims' needs unmet and offenders unrehabilitated.

- Romans 5:20a: "All that passing laws against sin did was produce more lawbreakers."

This verse highlights the limitations of merely punitive approaches, which can inadvertently perpetuate the cycle of harm rather than resolving it.

The Transformative Power of Restorative Justice

Addressing the Ripple Effect

Restorative justice seeks to interrupt the ripple effect of harm by addressing the needs of all affected parties and promoting healing and reconciliation. This approach aims to transform the negative contagion into a positive ripple effect of restoration.

- Principle: By focusing on healing and restoration, restorative justice can break the cycle of harm and create a ripple effect of positive change.

Meeting the Needs of Victims

Restorative justice prioritizes the needs of victims, providing them with opportunities to express their feelings, receive support, and be involved in the resolution process.

This holistic approach helps victims move beyond their pain and regain a sense of control over their lives.

- Romans 12:15: "Rejoice with those who rejoice; mourn with those who mourn."

By acknowledging and addressing the emotional and psychological needs of victims, restorative justice promotes genuine healing and recovery.

Rehabilitating Offenders

Restorative justice also focuses on the rehabilitation of offenders, encouraging them to take responsibility for their actions, make amends, and reintegrate into the community. This approach helps to prevent future harm and promotes personal transformation.

- 2 Corinthians 5:17: "Therefore, if anyone is in Christ, the new creation has come: The old has gone, the new is here!"

By offering offenders a pathway to redemption and transformation, restorative justice fosters a sense of hope and renewal.

Fostering Community Healing

Restorative justice involves the community in the healing process, promoting a collective sense of responsibility and support. This communal approach helps to rebuild trust and strengthen relationships.

- Galatians 6:2: "Carry each other's burdens, and in this way you will fulfill the law of Christ."

By fostering a supportive and cohesive community, restorative justice creates a ripple effect of positive change and resilience.

God's Future-Leaning Realm of Justice

The Role of Grace

In God's realm of justice, grace plays a central role. Romans 5:20b highlights the transformative power of grace, stating, "Sin doesn't have a chance in competition with the aggressive forgiveness we call grace."

- Romans 5:20b: "But where sin increased, grace increased all the more."

This aggressive forgiveness offers a radical departure from the retributive approach, emphasizing the power of grace to overcome sin and bring about true transformation.

The Power of Forgiveness

Forgiveness is a cornerstone of restorative justice and God's approach to justice. It involves releasing the burden of resentment and offering the possibility of redemption and reconciliation.

- Ephesians 4:32: "Be kind and compassionate to one another, forgiving each other, just as in Christ God forgave you."

Forgiveness not only frees the offender but also liberates the victim from the weight of the past, allowing for mutual healing and restoration.

Embracing a Future-Oriented Perspective

God's justice is future-oriented, focusing on the potential for transformation and renewal rather than being bound by past actions. This perspective encourages individuals and communities to look forward with hope and to work towards a better future.

- Philippians 3:13-14: "Brothers and sisters, I do not consider myself yet to have taken hold of it. But one thing I do: Forgetting what is behind and straining toward what is ahead, I press on toward the goal to win the prize for which God has called me heavenward in Christ Jesus."

By embracing a future-oriented perspective, restorative justice aligns with God's vision of hope, renewal, and continuous transformation.

Practical Steps for Implementing Restorative Justice

Creating Safe Spaces for Dialogue

Establish safe and confidential environments where victims, offenders, and community members can engage in open and honest dialogue. This helps to build trust and facilitates the healing process.

1. Facilitated Meetings: Organize meetings facilitated by trained mediators to ensure that all parties can express their feelings and perspectives in a safe and supportive setting.

2. Confidentiality Agreements: Implement confidentiality agreements to protect the privacy of those involved and to encourage open communication.

Providing Holistic Support

Offer comprehensive support services that address the emotional, psychological, and practical needs of victims and offenders.

1. Counseling Services: Provide access to professional counseling for victims and offenders to help them process their experiences and begin the healing journey.

2. Support Groups: Establish support groups where individuals can connect with others who have experienced similar situations and receive mutual support.

Promoting Accountability and Rehabilitation

Encourage offenders to take responsibility for their actions and to engage in rehabilitation programs that promote personal growth and transformation.

1. Accountability Plans: Develop individualized accountability plans that outline the steps offenders need to take to make amends and to prevent future harm.

2. Rehabilitation Programs: Offer programs that focus on skill-building, education, and personal development to help offenders reintegrate into the community as positive and contributing members.

Involving the Community

Engage the community in the restorative justice process, fostering a collective sense of responsibility and support.

1. Community Forums: Hold forums and town hall meetings to educate the community about restorative justice and to involve them in the healing process.

2. Volunteer Opportunities: Create opportunities for community members to volunteer in restorative justice initiatives, such as mentoring offenders or supporting victims.

Addressing Challenges and Maximizing Opportunities

Overcoming Skepticism

Skepticism about restorative justice can hinder its implementation. Overcoming this skepticism requires education, advocacy, and demonstrating the effectiveness of restorative justice.

1. Educational Campaigns: Launch educational campaigns to inform the community about the principles and benefits of restorative justice.

2. Showcasing Success Stories: Highlight success stories and testimonials from those who have benefited from restorative justice to build credibility and support.

Ensuring Equity and Fairness

It is essential to ensure that restorative justice processes are conducted fairly and equitably, without bias or discrimination.

1. Diverse Facilitators: Engage facilitators from diverse backgrounds to ensure that all perspectives are represented and respected.

2. Clear Guidelines: Establish clear guidelines and protocols to ensure consistency and fairness in the implementation of restorative justice.

Leveraging Partnerships

Collaborate with other organizations, institutions, and community groups to strengthen restorative justice initiatives and maximize their impact.

1. Partnership Agreements: Form partnerships with local organizations, schools, and justice systems to create a network of support for restorative justice.

2. Resource Sharing: Share resources, training, and expertise with partner organizations to enhance the effectiveness of restorative justice programs.

The Broader Implications for the Church

Reflecting the Gospel

By embracing restorative justice, the church reflects the core message of the gospel: grace, forgiveness, and reconciliation.

- 2 Corinthians 5:18-19: "All this is from God, who reconciled us to himself through Christ and gave us the ministry of reconciliation: that God was reconciling the world to himself in Christ, not counting people's sins against them. And he has committed to us the message of reconciliation."

The church's commitment to restorative justice demonstrates its dedication to living out the gospel in practical and transformative ways.

Building Stronger Communities

Restorative justice helps to build stronger, more resilient communities by promoting healing, trust, and mutual support.

- Ephesians 4:3: "Make every effort to keep the unity of the Spirit through the bond of peace."

A restorative culture enhances community cohesion and creates an environment where individuals can thrive.

Enhancing the

Church's Witness

A church that practices restorative justice serves as a powerful witness to the world, showcasing the transformative power of God's grace and the potential for renewal and reconciliation.

- Matthew 5:14-16: "You are the light of the world. A town built on a hill cannot be hidden. Neither do people light a lamp and put it under a bowl. Instead, they put it on its stand, and it gives light to everyone in the house. In the same way, let your light shine before others, that they may see your good deeds and glorify your Father in heaven."

Restorative justice enhances the church's witness, attracting others to the message of Christ and the hope of transformation.

The ripple effect caused by harm and crime can spread pain, mistrust, and negativity. Traditional justice processes that focus on punishment can exacerbate these effects. In contrast, restorative justice, grounded in the principles of grace, forgiveness, and reconciliation, offers a transformative approach. By meeting the needs of victims, rehabilitating offenders, and fostering community healing, restorative justice can create a positive ripple effect of restoration and renewal.

Understanding and applying these principles provides valuable insights for contemporary faith communities. By integrating restorative justice into their practices, churches can create environments where accountability, healing, and reconciliation thrive, reflecting the love and grace of Christ in powerful and transformative ways. Through this exploration, we aim to provide a comprehensive understanding of restorative justice as a vital aspect of Christian faith and practice, paving the way for a future-leaning realm of justice that embodies the heart of God's kingdom.

CHAPTER 09

THE INBREAKING OF DIVINE JUSTICE

Underlying Paul's interpretation of the Christ-event and the Gospel writers' presentation of the life and teaching of Jesus is an understanding of God's justice as a redemptive power that breaks into situations of oppression or need to put right what is wrong and restore relationships to their proper condition. Paul speaks of God's act of eschatological deliverance in the death and resurrection of Christ as a comprehensive work of justice-making that liberates oppressed humanity from the power of sin and death and from the guilt of actual transgression, bringing peace with God and reconciliation between former enemies. Jesus speaks of the inbreaking of divine justice as the coming of God's kingdom, which starts to put right what is wrong on earth, establishes a relationship of new intimacy between God and humanity, and calls into being a new community to live a transformed way of life in the midst of the old order. Distinctive of this life is the call to radical forgiveness of offenders and nonretaliation toward opponents, virtues taught and exemplified by Jesus himself and repeatedly affirmed throughout the New Testament. These virtues are not arbitrary requirements; they flow from the inherent character of divine justice itself.

God's Justice as Redemptive Power

Paul's Interpretation of the Christ-Event

Paul views the death and resurrection of Christ as a pivotal event in God's redemptive plan, a divine act of justice that transforms the human condition. This eschatological deliverance addresses both the systemic oppression of sin and death and the individual guilt of personal transgressions.

- Romans 3:21-24: "But now apart from the law the righteousness of God has been made known, to which the Law and the Prophets testify. This righteousness is given through faith in Jesus Christ to all who believe. There is no difference between Jew and Gentile, for all have sinned and fall short of the glory of God, and all are justified freely by his grace through the redemption that came by Christ Jesus."

Paul's message is clear: through Christ, God's justice liberates humanity, bringing peace and reconciliation. This comprehensive work of justice-making is not merely legalistic but deeply relational, restoring right relationships with God and among people.

The Gospel Writers' Presentation of Jesus

The Gospels present Jesus as the embodiment of divine justice, whose life and teachings inaugurate the kingdom of God. This inbreaking of divine justice begins the process of putting right what is wrong in the world and restoring relationships to their intended harmony.

- Luke 4:18-19: "The Spirit of the Lord is on me, because he has anointed me to proclaim good news to the poor. He has sent me to proclaim freedom for the prisoners and recovery of sight for the blind, to set the oppressed free, to proclaim the year of the Lord's favor."

Jesus' mission is one of liberation and restoration, bringing God's justice to bear on situations of need and oppression. This mission establishes a new intimacy between God and humanity and calls into being a community that reflects the values of the kingdom.

The Inbreaking of the Kingdom of God

Establishing Right Relationships

Jesus speaks of the kingdom of God as a reality that transforms human relationships. The inbreaking of divine justice through the kingdom starts to correct the wrongs on earth, creating new relationships marked by love, forgiveness, and mutual respect.

- Matthew 6:10: "Your kingdom come, your will be done, on earth as it is in heaven."

This prayer encapsulates the vision of the kingdom: a world where God's will is done, where justice, peace, and righteousness prevail.

The Call to Radical Forgiveness

One of the hallmarks of the kingdom is the call to radical forgiveness, a virtue that Jesus both taught and exemplified. This call challenges the natural human inclination toward retaliation and revenge.

- Matthew 18:21-22: "Then Peter came to Jesus and asked, 'Lord, how many times shall I forgive my brother or sister who sins against me? Up to seven times?' Jesus answered, 'I tell you, not seven times, but seventy-seven times.'"

Jesus' teaching on forgiveness is radical and countercultural, reflecting the transformative nature of the kingdom. It calls for a limitless willingness to forgive, mirroring the boundless grace of God.

Nonretaliation Toward Opponents

Alongside forgiveness, nonretaliation is a key virtue of the kingdom, exemplified by Jesus in his interactions with opponents and in his ultimate sacrifice on the cross.

- Matthew 5:38-39: "You have heard that it was said, 'Eye for eye, and tooth for tooth.' But I tell you, do not resist an evil person. If anyone slaps you on the right cheek, turn to them the other cheek also."

This teaching underscores the kingdom's ethic of nonviolence and grace, challenging believers to respond to hostility with love and forbearance.

Divine Justice in the New Testament

Paul's Vision of Eschatological Deliverance

Paul's letters repeatedly affirm the comprehensive nature of God's justice, which not only addresses sin but also reconciles and restores. This eschatological deliverance brings peace with God and heals divisions between people.

- Ephesians 2:14-16: "For he himself is our peace, who has made the two groups one and has destroyed the barrier, the dividing wall of hostility, by setting aside in his flesh the law with its commands and regulations. His purpose was to create in himself one new humanity out of the two, thus making peace, and in one body to reconcile both of them to God through the cross, by which he put to death their hostility."

Paul's vision is expansive, encompassing both individual transformation and communal reconciliation.

The New Community of the Kingdom

The New Testament calls believers to live out the values of the kingdom, forming a new community characterized by love, forgiveness, and justice. This community is a foretaste of the coming kingdom and a witness to the world.

- Colossians 3:12-14: "Therefore, as God's chosen people, holy and dearly loved, clothe yourselves with compassion, kindness, humility, gentleness and patience. Bear with each other and forgive one another if any of you has a grievance against someone. Forgive as the Lord forgave you. And over all these virtues put on love, which binds them all together in perfect unity."

The distinctive virtues of this new community flow from the inherent character of divine justice, reflecting the transformative power of God's redemptive work.

Practical Applications for Building a Restorative Culture

Educating on Kingdom Values

To build a restorative culture, it is essential to educate the church community about the values of the kingdom, emphasizing the importance of forgiveness, nonretaliation, and justice.

1. Sermons and Teachings: Regularly preach and teach on the themes of the kingdom, using Jesus' teachings and Paul's letters as foundational texts.

2. Bible Studies: Organize Bible studies that focus on the virtues of the kingdom, exploring their implications for personal and communal life.

Modeling Kingdom Ethics

Church leaders and members should model the ethics of the kingdom in their interactions, demonstrating radical forgiveness and nonretaliation in everyday situations.

1. Conflict Resolution: Apply principles of forgiveness and nonretaliation in resolving conflicts within the church, fostering a culture of grace and reconciliation.

2. Community Engagement: Engage with the broader community in ways that reflect the kingdom's values, promoting peace and justice in local and global contexts.

Creating Supportive Structures

Establish structures within the church that support the practice of kingdom values, providing resources and opportunities for members to live out these virtues.

1. Support Groups: Form support groups for those struggling with forgiveness, providing a safe space for sharing and healing.

2. Restorative Justice Teams: Develop teams trained in restorative justice practices to facilitate reconciliation processes and address harm within the community.

Addressing Challenges

Overcoming Resistance to Kingdom Values

Resistance to the radical ethics of the kingdom is common, both within and outside the church. Overcoming this resistance requires persistence, education, and the demonstration of these values in action.

1. Persistent Teaching: Continue to teach and emphasize the importance of kingdom values, even in the face of resistance.

2. Demonstration of Values: Demonstrate the transformative power of these values through real-life examples and testimonies.

Ensuring Equity and Fairness

It is essential to ensure that the application of kingdom values is fair and equitable, addressing the needs of all members and avoiding favoritism or bias.

1. Inclusive Practices: Develop inclusive practices that ensure all voices are heard and valued in the church community.

2. Equitable Processes: Establish equitable processes for addressing conflicts and harm, ensuring that justice is done in a fair and unbiased manner.

The Broader Implications for the Church

Reflecting God's Justice

By embracing the values of the kingdom, the church reflects God's justice, demonstrating the transformative power of grace and reconciliation to the world.

- Micah 6:8: "He has shown you, O mortal, what is good. And what does the Lord require of you? To act justly and to love mercy and to walk humbly with your God."

The church's commitment to these values enhances its witness and attracts others to the message of Christ.

Building a New Community

The church, as a community that embodies the values of the kingdom, serves as a model of what restored relationships can look like. This new community is a powerful testimony to the world of the redemptive power of God's justice.

- Acts 2:42-47: "They devoted themselves to the apostles' teaching and to fellowship, to the breaking of bread and to prayer. Everyone was

filled with awe at the many wonders and signs performed by the apostles. All the believers were together and had everything in common. They sold property and possessions to give to anyone who had need. Every day they continued to meet together in the temple courts. They broke bread in their homes and ate together with glad and sincere hearts, praising God and enjoying the favor of all the people. And the Lord added to their number daily those who were being saved."

This passage illustrates the transformative power of living out kingdom values, creating a vibrant and growing community.

Enhancing the Church's Witness

A church that practices the radical forgiveness, nonretaliation, and justice of the kingdom serves as a powerful witness to the world, showcasing the transformative power of God's grace.

- Matthew 5:14-16: "You are the light of the world. A town built on a hill cannot be hidden. Neither do people light a lamp and put it under a bowl. Instead, they put it on its stand, and it gives light to everyone in the house. In the same way, let your light shine before others, that they may see your good deeds and glorify your Father in heaven."

The church's commitment to these values enhances its witness and attracts others to the message of Christ.

Underlying Paul's interpretation of the Christ-event and the Gospel writers' presentation of the life and teaching of Jesus is an understanding of God's justice as a redemptive power that breaks into situations of oppression or need to put right what is wrong and restore relationships to their proper condition. Paul speaks of God's act of eschatological deliverance in the death and resurrection of Christ as a comprehensive work of justice-making that liberates oppressed humanity from the power of sin and death and from the guilt of actual transgression, bringing peace with God and reconciliation between former enemies. Jesus speaks of the inbreaking of divine justice as the coming of God's kingdom, which starts to put right what is wrong on earth, establishes a relationship of new intimacy between God and humanity, and calls into being a new community to live a transformed way of life in the midst of the old order. Distinctive of this life is the call to radical forgiveness of offenders and nonretaliation toward opponents, virtues taught and exemplified by Jesus himself and repeatedly affirmed throughout the New Testament. These virtues are not arbitrary requirements; they flow from the inherent character of divine justice itself.

By understanding and applying these principles, contemporary faith communities can build a restorative culture that reflects the love and grace of Christ, promoting healing, reconciliation, and justice in powerful and transformative ways. Through this exploration, we aim to provide a comprehensive understanding of restorative justice as a vital aspect of Christian faith and practice, paving the way for a future-leaning realm of justice that embodies the heart of God's kingdom.

CHAPTER 10

THE MEASURE OF HUMAN RIGHTEOUSNESS

God's saving justice is both the source and the measure of human righteousness. Biblical ethics expressly exclude the notion that we should deal with people only according to their merits, whether earned or unearned, or that we are simply to treat all people as their intrinsic worth deserves. Instead, the measure of justice is not corrective, distributive, or based on any other humanitarian standard, but rather a contributory justice—a helpful, redeeming, caring justice. This chapter explores the concept of contributory justice, examining how it is rooted in God's own righteousness, which stoops to conquer wrong and shapes human lives to its measure.

The Source and Measure of Human Righteousness

God's Saving Justice

God's saving justice, as revealed through the life, death, and resurrection of Jesus Christ, is the ultimate standard for human righteousness. This justice is characterized by its redemptive, transformative, and relational nature.

- Romans 1:17: "For in the gospel the righteousness of God is revealed—a righteousness that is by faith from first to last, just as it is written: 'The righteous will live by faith.'"

God's justice is not merely about punishing wrongdoing but about restoring right relationships and bringing about holistic redemption. It is an active, dynamic force that seeks to heal, redeem, and transform.

Contributory Justice

Contributory justice is a term that encapsulates this divine approach. Unlike corrective justice, which focuses on punishment, or distributive justice, which emphasizes fair distribution of resources, contributory justice is concerned with contributing positively to the well-being of others. It is a justice that helps, redeems, and cares.

- Micah 6:8: "He has shown you, O mortal, what is good. And what does the Lord require of you? To act justly and to love mercy and to walk humbly with your God."

This verse captures the essence of contributory justice—acting justly, loving mercy, and walking humbly with God, all of which contribute to the flourishing of others.

The Exclusion of Merit-Based Ethics

The Limits of Merit-Based Justice

Biblical ethics reject the idea that we should deal with people solely based on their merits. Merit-based justice, which rewards individuals according to their deeds, falls short of the redemptive justice that God models.

- Matthew 5:45: "He causes his sun to rise on the evil and the good, and sends rain on the righteous and the unrighteous."

God's grace and justice are not limited to those who deserve it by human standards. Instead, God's justice is inclusive, extending grace and mercy to all, regardless of merit.

The Call to Reflect God's Justice

Believers are called to reflect God's contributory justice in their interactions with others. This means going beyond mere fairness or merit and actively seeking to contribute to the well-being and redemption of others.

- Ephesians 4:32: "Be kind and compassionate to one another, forgiving each other, just as in Christ God forgave you."

This call to kindness, compassion, and forgiveness exemplifies contributory justice, as it seeks to heal and restore rather than to merely reward or punish.

Contributory Justice in Action

Practical Applications

Contributory justice can be applied in various aspects of community and personal life. It involves proactive efforts to care for and uplift others, reflecting God's redemptive love.

1. Supporting the Vulnerable: Contributory justice involves caring for those who are marginalized or vulnerable, providing them with the support and resources they need to thrive.

- James 1:27: "Religion that God our Father accepts as pure and faultless is this: to look after orphans and widows in their distress and to keep oneself from being polluted by the world."

2. Forgiving Offenders: This form of justice emphasizes forgiveness and reconciliation over retribution, offering offenders a path to redemption.

- Matthew 18:21-22: "Then Peter came to Jesus and asked, 'Lord, how many times shall I forgive my brother or sister who sins against me? Up to seven times?' Jesus answered, 'I tell you, not seven times, but seventy-seven times.'"

3. Promoting Fairness and Equity: While it goes beyond distributive justice, contributory justice still values fairness and equity, ensuring that everyone has the opportunity to contribute to and benefit from the community.

   - Acts 4:34-35: "There were no needy persons among them. For from time to time those who owned land or houses sold them, brought the money from the sales and put it at the apostles' feet, and it was distributed to anyone who had need."

The Role of the Church

The church plays a crucial role in modeling and promoting contributory justice. By creating environments where grace, mercy, and active care are the norm, churches can reflect God's justice to the broader community.

1. Community Outreach: Engage in outreach programs that address the needs of the community, providing support and resources to those in need.

   - Galatians 6:9-10: "Let us not become weary in doing good, for at the proper time we will reap a harvest if we do not give up. Therefore, as we have opportunity, let us do good to all people, especially to those who belong to the family of believers."

2. Restorative Practices: Implement restorative justice practices that focus on reconciliation and healing, rather than punishment.

- 2 Corinthians 5:18-19: "All this is from God, who reconciled us to himself through Christ and gave us the ministry of reconciliation: that God was reconciling the world to himself in Christ, not counting people's sins against them. And he has committed to us the message of reconciliation."

3. Education and Advocacy: Educate church members about the principles of contributory justice and advocate for policies that reflect these values in the wider society.

- Proverbs 31:8-9: "Speak up for those who cannot speak for themselves, for the rights of all who are destitute. Speak up and judge fairly; defend the rights of the poor and needy."

Challenges and Opportunities

Overcoming Barriers

Implementing contributory justice can encounter several challenges, including resistance to change and the ingrained nature of merit-based thinking. Overcoming these barriers requires intentional effort and a commitment to biblical principles.

1. Educational Efforts: Educate the community about the biblical basis for contributory justice and its importance in reflecting God's character.

- Romans 12:2: "Do not conform to the pattern of this world, but be transformed by the renewing of your mind. Then you will be able to test and approve what God's will is— his good, pleasing and perfect will."

2. Role Models: Highlight role models within the community who exemplify contributory justice, providing tangible examples for others to follow.

- 1 Corinthians 11:1: "Follow my example, as I follow the example of Christ."

Embracing Opportunities

The pursuit of contributory justice opens numerous opportunities for the church to make a positive impact, both within the congregation and in the broader community.

1. Building Stronger Communities: By practicing contributory justice, churches can build stronger, more resilient communities characterized by mutual support and care.

- Colossians 3:12-14: "Therefore, as God's chosen people, holy and dearly loved, clothe yourselves with compassion, kindness, humility, gentleness and patience. Bear with each other and forgive one another if any of you has a grievance against someone. Forgive as the Lord forgave you. And over all these virtues put on love, which binds them all together in perfect unity."

2.   Enhancing   Witness: Demonstrating   God's contributory justice enhances the church's witness, attracting others to the transformative message of the gospel.

- Matthew 5:16: "In the same way, let your light shine before others, that they may see your good deeds and glorify your Father in heaven."

God's saving justice is the source and measure of human righteousness, and it calls for a contributory justice— a justice that is helpful, redeeming, and caring. This approach is distinct from merit-based, corrective, or distributive justice, as it reflects the inherent character of divine justice that seeks to restore and redeem. By embracing contributory justice, believers can live out the principles of God's kingdom, fostering communities marked by grace, mercy, and mutual support. Understanding and applying these principles provides valuable insights for contemporary faith communities, helping them to reflect the transformative power of God's justice in all aspects of life. Through this exploration, we aim to provide a comprehensive understanding of contributory justice as a vital aspect of

Christian faith and practice, paving the way for a justice that truly reflects the heart of God.

CHAPTER 11

NEW TESTAMENT RESTORATIVE PRACTICES

The New Testament, particularly the Gospel of Matthew, provides a framework for restorative justice practices that address social injustices and empower those marginalized by societal structures. In Matthew 18, Jesus outlines a three-phase process for resolving harms and offenses designed to dignify those who have been harmed and restore those who have done the harm. This chapter explores the social context of Matthew's writings, the restorative justice practices he presents, and the implications for contemporary faith communities.

The Social Context of Matthew's Writings

Social Stratification and Marginalization

In the first-century Mediterranean world, social stratification was pervasive, creating clear divisions between the rich and powerful and the poor and marginalized. Those who were victimized by social structures and injustices often found themselves disempowered and voiceless.

- Historical Background: Understanding the historical and social context of Matthew's Gospel is crucial for appreciating the radical nature of Jesus' teachings on restorative justice. The Roman Empire's hierarchical structure and the Jewish religious elite's power dynamics often left the vulnerable further marginalized.

Jesus' Ministry to the Marginalized

Jesus' ministry was characterized by his solidarity with the least and the lost, challenging the existing social order and advocating for the dignity and restoration of all individuals.

- Luke 4:18-19: "The Spirit of the Lord is on me, because he has anointed me to proclaim good news to the poor. He has sent me to proclaim freedom for the prisoners and recovery of sight for the blind, to set the oppressed free, to proclaim the year of the Lord's favor."

Jesus' mission was fundamentally restorative, seeking to heal, liberate, and restore those oppressed by social and spiritual forces.

The Three-Phase Process in Matthew 18

Phase One: Private Confrontation

The first phase of Jesus' process for resolving offenses involves a private confrontation between the parties involved.

- Matthew 18:15: "If your brother or sister sins, go and point out their fault, just between the two of you. If they listen to you, you have won them over."

This step emphasizes the importance of addressing issues directly and privately, aiming for reconciliation without escalating the conflict.

Practical Application

1. Direct Communication: Encourage individuals to approach those who have wronged them privately and respectfully, seeking to resolve the issue without involving others.

2. Empathy and Understanding: Foster an environment where empathy and understanding are prioritized, helping individuals to see the perspective of the other party.

Phase Two: Small Group Involvement

If the private confrontation does not resolve the issue, the second phase involves bringing one or two others into the conversation to help mediate and support reconciliation.

- Matthew 18:16: "But if they will not listen, take one or two others along, so that 'every matter may be established by the testimony of two or three witnesses.'"

This step provides additional perspectives and support, aiming to reach a fair and just resolution.

Practical Application

1. Mediation Teams: Form mediation teams within the church trained to facilitate conflict resolution, providing neutral support to those involved in disputes.

2. Building Trust: Ensure that the individuals chosen to mediate are trusted by both parties and committed to seeking a just and peaceful resolution.

Phase Three: Community Involvement

If the issue remains unresolved, the final phase involves bringing the matter before the broader community for resolution.

- Matthew 18:17: "If they still refuse to listen, tell it to the church; and if they refuse to listen even to the church, treat them as you would a pagan or a tax collector."

This step emphasizes the community's role in maintaining justice and harmony, holding individuals accountable while seeking restoration.

Practical Application

1. Community Forums: Establish forums where unresolved conflicts can be brought before the community, ensuring that the process is fair, transparent, and aimed at reconciliation.

2. Support Systems: Create support systems within the community to help individuals affected by the conflict, providing counseling and resources to facilitate healing.

The 'Seventy-Times-Seven' Restorative Justice Liturgy

Radical Forgiveness

In the second half of Matthew 18, Jesus underscores the importance of radical forgiveness, presenting it as a fundamental aspect of restorative justice.

- Matthew 18:21-22: "Then Peter came to Jesus and asked, 'Lord, how many times shall I forgive my brother or sister who sins against me? Up to seven times?' Jesus answered, 'I tell you, not seven times, but seventy-seven times.'"

This call to limitless forgiveness challenges the retributive justice mindset and emphasizes the transformative power of grace.

Practical Application

1. Teaching Forgiveness: Incorporate teachings on radical forgiveness into sermons and Bible studies, helping the community to understand and practice this crucial aspect of restorative justice.

2. Forgiveness Workshops: Offer workshops focused on the process and importance of forgiveness, providing practical tools and support for those struggling to forgive.

Nonretaliation and Grace

Jesus contrasts the 'seventy-times-seven' restorative justice liturgy with the retributive justice liturgy of the rich and powerful, who live in a fearful, dog-eat-dog world.

- Matthew 18:23-35: Jesus tells the parable of the unforgiving servant, illustrating the dire consequences of failing to extend the grace that one has received.

This parable highlights the expectation that those who have experienced God's grace must extend it to others, rejecting retaliation and embracing forgiveness.

Practical Application

1. Modeling Grace: Encourage church leaders and members to model grace and nonretaliation in their interactions, setting an example for others to follow.

2. Conflict Resolution Policies: Develop conflict resolution policies that prioritize grace and restoration over punishment and retribution.

The Curse of Lamech and Restorative Justice

The Curse of Lamech

The story of Lamech in Genesis 4:23-24 represents the cycle of vengeance and retribution that restorative justice seeks to break.

- Genesis 4:23-24: "Lamech said to his wives, 'Adah and Zillah, listen to me; wives of Lamech, hear my words. I have killed a man for wounding me, a young man for injuring me. If Cain is avenged seven times, then Lamech seventy-seven times.'"

Lamech's boast of excessive vengeance contrasts sharply with Jesus' call to forgive seventy-seven times, highlighting the destructive nature of retributive justice.

Breaking the Cycle of Vengeance

Restorative justice, as exemplified by Jesus, offers a way to break the cycle of vengeance and create a culture of peace and reconciliation.

- Romans 12:17-21: "Do not repay anyone evil for evil. Be careful to do what is right in the eyes of everyone. If it is possible, as far as it depends on you, live at peace with everyone. Do not take revenge, my dear friends, but leave room for God's wrath, for it is written: 'It is mine to avenge; I will repay,' says the Lord. On the contrary: 'If your enemy is hungry, feed him; if he is thirsty, give him something to drink. In doing this, you will heap burning coals on his head.' Do not be overcome by evil, but overcome evil with good."

This passage underscores the transformative power of overcoming evil with good, a core principle of restorative justice.

Practical Application

1. Promoting Peace: Foster a culture of peace within the church, encouraging members to resolve conflicts through dialogue and understanding rather than retaliation.

2. Educational Programs: Develop educational programs that teach the principles of restorative justice, helping the community to understand and embrace these values.

Matthew 18 provides a comprehensive framework for restorative justice that addresses social injustices and empowers those marginalized by societal structures. The three-phase process for resolving harms and offenses is designed to dignify those who have been harmed and restore those who have done the harming. By embracing the 'seventy-times-seven' restorative justice liturgy, believers can reject the retributive justice mindset and break the cycle of vengeance exemplified by Lamech.

Understanding and applying these principles provides valuable insights for contemporary faith communities. By integrating restorative justice into their practices, churches can create environments where dignity, restoration, and reconciliation thrive, reflecting the love and grace of Christ in powerful and transformative ways. Through this exploration, we aim to provide a comprehensive understanding of New Testament restorative practices as a vital aspect of Christian faith and practice, paving the way for a justice that truly embodies the heart of God's kingdom.

CHAPTER 12

THE CRUCIFORM NATURE OF RESTORATIVE JUSTICE

Restorative justice in the New Testament is deeply rooted in the concept of solidarity and vulnerability, exemplified by Jesus and echoed in the writings of Paul. This chapter explores how the breaking down of the wall of hostility in Ephesians 2 and the nonviolent usage of God's armor within a retributive world illustrate this principle. Additionally, it examines how 2 Corinthians highlights the role of Christians as ambassadors of reconciliation, emphasizing the cost of discipleship and the pattern of vulnerability and re-empowerment that underpins restorative dialogue. The cruciform nature of restorative justice gives new life precisely because strength is perfected through weakness.

Breaking Down the Wall of Hostility

Ephesians 2: The Wall of Hostility

In Ephesians 2, Paul describes the breaking down of the wall of hostility between Jews and Gentiles, achieved through the reconciling work of Christ. This passage highlights the transformative power of Christ's peace in creating a new, unified humanity.

- Ephesians 2:14-16: "For he himself is our peace, who has made the two groups one and has destroyed the barrier, the dividing wall of hostility, by setting aside in his flesh the law with its commands and regulations. His purpose was to create in himself one new humanity out of the two, thus making peace, and in one body to reconcile both of them to God through the cross, by which he put to death their hostility."

This passage illustrates how Christ's sacrificial love breaks down barriers and fosters reconciliation, creating a new community grounded in peace and unity.

Nonviolent Usage of God's Armor

Paul's exhortation to put on the full armor of God in Ephesians 6 emphasizes the nonviolent nature of spiritual warfare within a retributive world. This armor equips believers to stand firm against evil without resorting to violence.

- Ephesians 6:13-17: "Therefore put on the full armor of God, so that when the day of evil comes, you may be able to stand your ground, and after you have done everything, to stand. Stand firm then, with the belt of truth buckled around your waist, with the breastplate of righteousness in place, and with your feet fitted with the readiness that comes from the gospel of peace. In addition to all this, take up the shield of faith, with which you can extinguish all the flaming arrows of the evil one. Take the helmet of salvation and the sword of the Spirit, which is the word of God."

The imagery of God's armor underscores the principles of truth, righteousness, peace, faith, salvation, and the Spirit, all of which are crucial for engaging in restorative justice.

Ambassadors of Reconciliation

2 Corinthians 5: Ambassadors of Reconciliation

In 2 Corinthians 5, Paul describes believers as ambassadors of reconciliation, entrusted with the ministry of reconciliation. This role involves representing Christ and working to restore relationships between God and humanity and among people.

- 2 Corinthians 5:18-20: "All this is from God, who reconciled us to himself through Christ and gave us the ministry of reconciliation: that God was reconciling the world to himself in Christ, not counting people's sins against them. And he has committed to us the message of reconciliation.

We are therefore Christ's ambassadors, as though God were making his appeal through us. We implore you on Christ's behalf: Be reconciled to God."

As ambassadors, believers are called to embody and promote the reconciling work of Christ, fostering peace and unity in their communities.

The Cost of Discipleship

In 2 Corinthians 6, Paul outlines the hardships and challenges faced by those who follow Christ, emphasizing the cost of discipleship and the solidarity required with the dishonored and disempowered.

- 2 Corinthians 6:3-10: "We put no stumbling block in anyone's path so that our ministry will not be discredited. Rather, as servants of God we commend ourselves in every way: in great endurance; in troubles, hardships, and distresses; in beatings, imprisonments, and riots; in hard work, sleepless nights and hunger; in purity, understanding, patience, and kindness; in the Holy Spirit and sincere love; in truthful speech and the power of God; with weapons of righteousness in the right hand and in the left; through glory and dishonor, bad report and good report; genuine, yet regarded as impostors; known, yet regarded as unknown; dying, and yet we live on; beaten, and yet not killed; sorrowful, yet always rejoicing; poor, yet making many rich; having nothing, and yet possessing everything."

Paul's ministry exemplifies the cruciform nature of discipleship—embracing vulnerability and suffering to bring about reconciliation and new life.

The Pattern of Vulnerability and Re-Empowerment

Solidarity with the Marginalized

Jesus' and Paul's ministries both emphasize solidarity with the marginalized, reflecting God's initiative to make atonement in solidarity with humanity. This pattern of vulnerability and re-empowerment is central to restorative justice.

- Philippians 2:5-8: "In your relationships with one another, have the same mindset as Christ Jesus: Who, being in very nature God, did not consider equality with God something to be used to his advantage; rather, he made himself nothing by taking the very nature of a servant, being made in human likeness. And being found in appearance as a man, he humbled himself by becoming obedient to death— even death on a cross!"

Jesus' willingness to become vulnerable and suffer for the sake of humanity sets the ultimate example of restorative justice.

Restorative Dialogue

Restorative dialogue, premised on the pattern of vulnerability and re-empowerment, is a crucial component of restorative justice. It involves open, honest communication that seeks to heal and restore relationships.

- James 5:16: "Therefore confess your sins to each other and pray for each other so that you may be healed. The prayer of a righteous person is powerful and effective."

Confession and prayer within a community foster a culture of vulnerability and mutual support, essential for restorative dialogue.

Strength Perfected Through Weakness

The Cruciform Nature of New Life

The cruciform (cross-shaped) nature of new life in Christ involves embracing weakness and vulnerability as pathways to true strength and empowerment.

2 Corinthians 12:9-10: "But he said to me, 'My grace is sufficient for you, for my power is made perfect in weakness.' Therefore, I will boast all the more gladly about my weaknesses, so that Christ's power may rest on me. That is why, for Christ's sake, I delight in weaknesses, in insults, in hardships, in persecutions, in difficulties. For when I am weak, then I am strong."

This paradoxical truth underscores the transformative power of God's grace, which brings strength out of weakness and life out of death.

Practical Applications

1. Embracing Vulnerability: Encourage individuals to embrace vulnerability in their interactions, fostering deeper connections and mutual support.

- Example: Create safe spaces for sharing personal struggles and experiences, promoting a culture of openness and authenticity.

2. Empowering the Disempowered: Develop programs and initiatives that empower marginalized individuals, providing resources and opportunities for growth and development.

- Example: Establish mentorship programs that pair community members with marginalized individuals, offering guidance and support.

3. Fostering Restorative Dialogue: Facilitate restorative dialogue sessions that allow for open, honest communication and the resolution of conflicts.

- Example: Organize restorative justice circles where participants can share their experiences and work together to find healing and resolution.

The New Testament provides a powerful framework for restorative justice rooted in the cruciform nature of Christ's ministry and the teachings of Paul. By breaking down the wall of hostility, embracing nonviolent resistance, and becoming ambassadors of reconciliation, believers are called to live out a justice that is both vulnerable and empowering. Restorative dialogue, grounded in this pattern of vulnerability and re-empowerment, offers new life and healing to individuals and communities. Strength is perfected through weakness, reflecting the transformative power of God's grace.

Understanding and applying these principles provides valuable insights for contemporary faith communities. By integrating restorative justice into their practices, churches can create environments where dignity, restoration, and reconciliation thrive, reflecting the love and grace of Christ in powerful and transformative ways. Through this exploration, we aim to provide a comprehensive understanding of New Testament restorative practices as a vital aspect of Christian faith and practice, paving the way for a justice that truly embodies the heart of God's kingdom.

CHAPTER 13

AMBASSADORS OF RECONCILIATION

Witnessing to the Restorative Justice of God (2 Corinthians 5:16-21)

In 2 Corinthians 5:16-21, Paul presents a compelling vision of believers as ambassadors of reconciliation, entrusted with the ministry of reconciliation. This passage highlights the transformative power of God's restorative justice, calling Christians to witness to this divine justice through their lives and actions. This chapter explores the implications of being ambassadors of reconciliation, emphasizing the role of Christians in embodying and promoting God's restorative justice.

The Ministry of Reconciliation

A New Perspective on Humanity

Paul begins by challenging believers to adopt a new perspective, no longer viewing people from a worldly point of view but recognizing the transformative potential of every individual in Christ.

- 2 Corinthians 5:16: "So from now on we regard no one from a worldly point of view. Though we once regarded Christ in this way, we do so no longer."

This new perspective is foundational for restorative justice, which seeks to see individuals not merely in terms of their past actions but as new creations with the potential for transformation and reconciliation.

Practical Application

1. Renewed Vision: Encourage church members to see others through the lens of grace and potential, fostering an environment of acceptance and hope.

- Example: Share testimonies of transformed lives to illustrate the power of seeing others as new creations in Christ.

The New Creation

Paul emphasizes that in Christ, individuals become new creations, leaving behind the old and embracing the new.

- 2 Corinthians 5:17: "Therefore, if anyone is in Christ, the new creation has come: 'The old has gone, the new is here!'"

This transformative reality underscores the restorative justice of God, which brings about new life and new possibilities.

Practical Application

1. Celebrating Transformation: Create opportunities to celebrate and acknowledge the transformative work of Christ in individuals' lives.

- Example: Hold services or events where members can share their stories of transformation and renewal.

The Ministry of Reconciliation Entrusted to Believers

Paul declares that God has reconciled us to Himself through Christ and given us the ministry of reconciliation.

- 2 Corinthians 5:18-19: "All this is from God, who reconciled us to himself through Christ and gave us the ministry of reconciliation: that God was reconciling the world to himself in Christ, not counting people's sins against them. And he has committed to us the message of reconciliation."

This passage highlights the divine initiative in reconciliation and the responsibility of believers to carry forward this ministry.

Practical Application

1. Equipping for Ministry: Provide training and resources to equip believers for the ministry of reconciliation.

- Example: Offer workshops on conflict resolution, forgiveness, and restorative justice principles.

Ambassadors for Christ

The Role of Ambassadors

Paul uses the metaphor of ambassadors to describe the role of believers, emphasizing their responsibility to represent Christ and His message of reconciliation to the world.

- 2 Corinthians 5:20: "We are therefore Christ's ambassadors, as though God were making his appeal through us. We implore you on Christ's behalf: Be reconciled to God."

As ambassadors, Christians are called to embody the values and principles of God's restorative justice, serving as agents of reconciliation in their communities.

Practical Application

1. Ambassador Training: Develop programs that train believers to serve as ambassadors of reconciliation in various contexts.

- Example: Create a mentorship program where experienced leaders mentor new believers in the principles of restorative justice and reconciliation.

The Appeal of Reconciliation

Paul's urgent appeal for reconciliation underscores the transformative power of God's justice and the believer's role in promoting it.

- 2 Corinthians 5:21: "God made him who had no sin to be sin for us, so that in him we might become the righteousness of God."

This verse encapsulates the gospel message, highlighting the depth of God's love and the extent of His restorative justice.

Practical Application

1. Gospel-Centered Outreach: Focus outreach efforts on sharing the message of reconciliation, emphasizing the transformative power of God's justice.

- Example: Organize community events that promote reconciliation and healing, providing opportunities for individuals to experience God's restorative justice.

Witnessing to Restorative Justice

Embodying Restorative Justice

Believers are called to embody the principles of restorative justice in their daily lives, reflecting God's love, grace, and forgiveness.

- Colossians 3:12-14: "Therefore, as God's chosen people, holy and dearly loved, clothe yourselves with compassion, kindness, humility, gentleness, and patience.

Bear with each other and forgive one another if any of you has a grievance against someone. Forgive as the Lord forgave you. And over all these virtues put on love, which binds them all together in perfect unity."

By embodying these virtues, Christians can serve as living witnesses to the power of God's restorative justice.

Practical Application

1. Modeling Virtues: Encourage church leaders and members to model virtues such as compassion, kindness, and forgiveness in their interactions.

- Example: Highlight examples of individuals who exemplify these virtues, providing inspiration and practical guidance.

Promoting Reconciliation

Promoting reconciliation involves actively working to heal broken relationships and restore community.

- Romans 12:18: "If it is possible, as far as it depends on you, live at peace with everyone."

This commitment to peace and reconciliation is central to the mission of believers as ambassadors of God's justice.

Practical Application

1. Conflict Resolution Initiatives: Establish initiatives that focus on resolving conflicts and promoting reconciliation within the community.

- Example: Create a conflict resolution team that offers mediation and support for individuals and groups in conflict.

Advocacy and Justice

Witnessing God's restorative justice also involves advocating for justice and addressing systemic issues that contribute to oppression and injustice.

- Isaiah 1:17: "Learn to do right; seek justice. Defend the oppressed. Take up the cause of the fatherless; plead the case of the widow."

Advocacy for justice is a crucial aspect of the ministry of reconciliation, reflecting God's heart for the marginalized and oppressed.

Practical Application

1. Justice Advocacy: Engage in advocacy efforts that address systemic injustices and promote equitable treatment for all individuals.

- Example: Partner with local organizations to advocate for policy changes that promote justice and reconciliation.

Challenges and Opportunities

Overcoming Resistance

Implementing restorative justice and reconciliation efforts can encounter resistance from those who are accustomed to retributive justice or who harbor unforgiveness.

1. Educational Efforts: Provide education on the biblical principles of restorative justice and reconciliation to address misconceptions and resistance.

- Example: Host seminars and discussion groups that explore the theological foundations and practical applications of restorative justice.

Embracing Opportunities

The call to be ambassadors of reconciliation opens numerous opportunities for believers to make a positive impact in their communities and beyond.

1. Community Engagement: Actively engage with the community to promote reconciliation and justice, building relationships and fostering trust.

- Example: Organize community service projects that address local needs and promote a culture of reconciliation.

The Broader Implications for the Church

Reflecting God's Justice

By embracing the ministry of reconciliation, the church reflects the transformative power of God's justice, serving as a beacon of hope and healing.

- Matthew 5:14-16: "You are the light of the world. A town built on a hill cannot be hidden. Neither do people light a lamp and put it under a bowl. Instead, they put it on its stand, and it gives light to everyone in the house. In the same way, let your light shine before others, that they may see your good deeds and glorify your Father in heaven."

The church's commitment to restorative justice enhances its witness and attracts others to the message of Christ.

Building a Reconciled Community

The church, as a reconciled community, serves as a model of what restored relationships can look like, demonstrating the power of God's justice to transform lives and communities.

- Ephesians 4:3: "Make every effort to keep the unity of the Spirit through the bond of peace."

A reconciled community is a powerful testimony to the world of the redemptive power of God's justice.

In 2 Corinthians 5:16-21, Paul presents a vision of believers as ambassadors of reconciliation, entrusted with the ministry of reconciliation. This passage highlights the transformative power of God's restorative justice, calling Christians to witness to this divine justice through their lives and actions. By adopting a new perspective, embracing the role of ambassadors, and embodying restorative justice, believers can make a profound impact in their communities.

Understanding and applying these principles provides valuable insights for contemporary faith communities. By integrating restorative justice into their practices, churches can create environments where dignity, restoration, and reconciliation thrive, reflecting the love and grace of Christ in powerful and transformative ways. Through this exploration, we aim to provide a comprehensive understanding of the role of ambassadors of reconciliation as a vital aspect of Christian faith and practice, paving the way for a justice that truly embodies the heart of God's kingdom.

CHAPTER 14

A BIBLICAL RESTORATIVE AND RETRIBUTIVE JUSTICE

The Church and State Conflict Resolution Approach According to 1 Corinthians 6:1-11

This chapter seeks to identify biblical principles in 1 Corinthians 6:1-11 that define a restorative and retributive justice approach to addressing conflicts and divisions within the church and the community. The study has two main objectives: to conduct an exegetical study of 1 Corinthians 6:1-11 and to set biblical guidelines that define the complementarity of restorative justice with retributive justice. The chapter argues that Paul's model of church conflict resolution in 1 Corinthians 6:1-11 is appropriate for adopting a complementary approach that integrates the state's retributive judicial system with restorative justice principles.

Exegetical Study of 1 Corinthians 6:1-11

Context and Background

Paul's letter to the Corinthians addresses various issues within the church, including divisions, immorality, and litigation among believers. In 1 Corinthians 6:1-11, Paul specifically rebukes the Corinthians for taking their disputes before secular courts rather than resolving them within the church community.

- 1 Corinthians 6:1-2: "If any of you has a dispute with another, do you dare to take it before the ungodly for judgment instead of before the Lord's people? Or do you not know that the Lord's people will judge the world? And if you are to judge the world, are you not competent to judge trivial cases?"

Paul's emphasis is on the competence and responsibility of the church to handle internal disputes, reflecting a preference for a restorative approach grounded in Christian values.

Key Principles

1. Internal Resolution: Paul advocates for resolving disputes within the church rather than seeking judgment from secular courts.

- 1 Corinthians 6:3-4: "Do you not know that we will judge angels? How much more the things of this life! Therefore, if you have disputes about such matters, do you ask for a ruling from those whose way of life is scorned in the church?"

2. Wise Judgment: Paul stresses the importance of wise and mature believers acting as judges in disputes, ensuring that decisions reflect Christian principles of justice and reconciliation.

- 1 Corinthians 6:5: "I say this to shame you. Is it possible that there is nobody among you wise enough to judge a dispute between believers?"

3. Community Integrity: By handling disputes internally, the church maintains its integrity and witness to the outside world, avoiding public scandals that could undermine its testimony.

- 1 Corinthians 6:6: "But instead, one brother takes another to court—and this in front of unbelievers!"

Deductive Analysis

Through a deductive analysis of the text, several key judiciary principles emerge that can be applied to both the church and state justice systems:

1. Emphasis on Reconciliation: The primary goal is reconciliation rather than punishment, reflecting the restorative justice model.

2. Utilization of Wisdom: Disputes should be resolved by wise and mature individuals within the community who can provide fair and just resolutions.

3. Maintaining Integrity: Handling conflicts within the community preserves the integrity and witness of the church.

Complementarity of Restorative and Retributive Justice

Integrating Restorative and Retributive Justice

Paul's approach in 1 Corinthians 6:1-11 provides a model for integrating restorative and retributive justice, highlighting the need for both reconciliation and accountability.

- Restorative Justice: Focuses on healing and restoring relationships, emphasizing reconciliation and the reintegration of offenders into the community.

- Retributive Justice: Focuses on accountability and the fair application of consequences for wrongdoing, ensuring justice is served.

Biblical Guidelines

The study suggests several biblical guidelines for integrating these approaches:

1. Conflict Resolution by Wise Church Members: Disputes between believers should be handled by wise and

mature church members who can administer both restorative and retributive justice based on biblical principles.

- 1 Corinthians 6:5: "Is it possible that there is nobody among you wise enough to judge a dispute between believers?"

2. Adoption of Conflict Resolution Models: The church and state justice systems should adopt conflict resolution models that incorporate both restorative and retributive justice, ensuring comprehensive and just outcomes.

- 1 Corinthians 6:1-2: "If any of you has a dispute with another, do you dare to take it before the ungodly for judgment instead of before the Lord's people?"

3. Intentional Discipleship: The church should intentionally disciple members to maturity, identifying and appointing wise believers who can serve as judges and administrators of justice.

- Ephesians 4:11-13: "So Christ himself gave the apostles, the prophets, the evangelists, the pastors and teachers, to equip his people for works of service, so that the body of Christ may be built up until we all reach unity in the faith and in the knowledge of the Son of God and become mature, attaining to the whole measure of the fullness of Christ."

Historical Grammatical Criticism and Socio-Scientific Criticism

Understanding the Original Message

The study employs historical grammatical criticism to understand the original message of the text in its ancient Jewish and Greco-Roman context. This method involves analyzing the historical, cultural, and linguistic aspects of the text to uncover its intended meaning.

- Historical Context: Understanding the role of secular courts and the importance of communal integrity in the early Christian context.

- Grammatical Analysis: Analyzing the specific language and structure of the text to understand Paul's instructions and their implications.

Socio-Scientific Criticism

Socio-scientific criticism provides additional insights by examining the social and cultural dynamics at play in the early Christian community.

- Social Dynamics: Examining how social stratification, honor-shame culture, and community cohesion influenced Paul's approach to conflict resolution.

- Cultural Context: Understanding the Greco-Roman legal system and its contrasts with the values of the Christian community.

Recommendations

Based on the exegetical study and analysis, the following recommendations are made:

1. Conflict Resolution by Wise Church Members: Conflicts between believers should be handled by wise and mature church members who can administer both restorative and retributive justice based on biblical principles.

2. Adoption of Conflict Resolution Models: The church and state justice systems should adopt models that incorporate both restorative and retributive justice, ensuring comprehensive and just outcomes.

3. Intentional Discipleship: The church should disciple members to maturity, identifying and appointing wise believers to serve as judges and administrators of justice, thus ensuring the application of equitable retributive and restorative justice.

The Concept of "Biblical Gacaca"

The concept of "Biblical Gacaca" emerges as a judiciary system that embodies both retributive and restorative justice in the church and state. This system, informed by biblical principles, aims to resolve conflicts and promote justice and reconciliation within the community.

- Gacaca Courts: Inspired by traditional Rwandan Gacaca courts, which focused on community-based justice and reconciliation after the genocide.

- Biblical Principles: Incorporating the biblical principles of reconciliation, accountability, and community integrity to create a justice system that reflects God's justice.

Implementing Biblical Gacaca

1. Community-Based Justice: Establish community-based justice systems within the church that focus on reconciliation and accountability.

2. Training and Resources: Provide training and resources for church members to understand and implement the principles of Biblical Gacaca.

3. Collaboration with State: Encourage collaboration between the church and state to integrate restorative and retributive justice principles in broader judicial processes.

This chapter has explored the principles of restorative and retributive justice in 1 Corinthians 6:1-11, highlighting the importance of resolving conflicts within the church community. By conducting an exegetical study and setting biblical guidelines, it has demonstrated the complementarity of these justice approaches and the potential for integrating them in both church and state justice systems. The concept of "Biblical Gacaca" offers a model for a judiciary system that embodies these principles, promoting justice, reconciliation, and community integrity.

Understanding and applying these principles provides valuable insights for contemporary faith communities and justice systems. By integrating restorative and retributive justice, churches and states can create environments where justice, reconciliation, and restoration thrive, reflecting the love and grace of Christ in powerful and transformative ways. Through this exploration, we aim to provide a comprehensive understanding of the biblical approach to conflict resolution and justice, paving the way for a justice that truly embodies the heart of God's kingdom.

THE TRANSFORMATIVE POWER OF RESTORATIVE JUSTICE

Restorative justice, as outlined in 1st and 2nd Corinthians, offers a powerful and biblical framework for addressing harm, fostering reconciliation, and promoting holistic healing within communities. Through an in-depth exploration of Paul's teachings and the principles of restorative justice, this study has highlighted the profound impact these practices can have on individuals and communities. By embracing these principles, believers can reflect the heart of the gospel and the ministry of reconciliation entrusted to them.

The Heart of the Gospel

At the core of the gospel message is the transformative power of reconciliation. Paul's letters to the Corinthians emphasize that through Christ, God has reconciled the world to Himself and has given believers the ministry of reconciliation. This divine initiative not only restores broken relationships but also calls believers to actively participate in this restorative work.

- 2 Corinthians 5:18-19: "All this is from God, who reconciled us to himself through Christ and gave us the ministry of reconciliation: that God was reconciling the world to himself in Christ, not counting people's sins against them. And he has committed to us the message of reconciliation."

This passage encapsulates the essence of restorative justice: a commitment to repairing harm, restoring relationships, and promoting peace and unity within the community.

Principles of Restorative Justice in 1st and 2nd Corinthians

Throughout 1st and 2nd Corinthians, Paul provides a framework for restorative justice that emphasizes accountability, forgiveness, and reconciliation. Key principles include:

1. Accountability and Responsibility: Offenders are encouraged to acknowledge their actions and take responsibility for the harm caused, reflecting the importance of justice and repentance.

- 1 Corinthians 5:3-5: Paul instructs the church to address the issue of sexual immorality and take necessary steps to restore the offender while protecting the community's integrity.

2. Forgiveness and Grace: Believers are called to extend forgiveness and grace, mirroring the forgiveness they have received from God.

- 2 Corinthians 2:6-8: Paul urges the community to forgive and comfort a repentant offender, reaffirming their love and support.

3. Reconciliation and Restoration: The ultimate goal of restorative justice is the restoration of relationships and the reintegration of individuals into the community.

- 2 Corinthians 5:20: "We are therefore Christ's ambassadors, as though God were making his appeal through us. We implore you on Christ's behalf: Be reconciled to God."

The Role of the Church

The church plays a crucial role in modeling and promoting restorative justice. By adopting restorative practices, the church can create a culture of healing and reconciliation that reflects the values of the kingdom of God.

- Conflict Resolution: Encouraging the resolution of conflicts within the community through dialogue, mediation, and restorative processes.

- 1 Corinthians 6:1-5: Paul admonishes the Corinthians to resolve disputes among themselves rather than taking them to secular courts, highlighting the church's responsibility in conflict resolution.

- Support and Healing: Providing support for both victims and offenders, ensuring that the needs of all parties are addressed and that healing can occur.

- Galatians 6:1-2: "Brothers and sisters, if someone is caught in a sin, you who live by the Spirit should restore that person gently. But watch yourselves, or you also may be tempted. Carry each other's burdens, and in this way you will fulfill the law of Christ."

- Education and Discipleship: Educating and discipling church members in the principles of restorative justice, equipping them to live out these values in their daily lives.   - Ephesians 4:11-13: Paul emphasizes the importance of equipping the saints for the work of ministry, building up the body of Christ to maturity.

Transformative Impact

The implementation of restorative justice principles has the potential to transform individuals and communities profoundly. By focusing on healing rather than punishment, restorative justice fosters environments where people can experience genuine change and reconciliation.

1. Personal Transformation: Individuals who engage in restorative justice processes often experience deep personal growth, as they confront the impact of their actions and seek to make amends.

- 2 Corinthians 7:10-11: "Godly sorrow brings repentance that leads to salvation and leaves no regret, but worldly sorrow brings death. See what this godly sorrow has produced in you: what earnestness, what eagerness to clear yourselves, what indignation, what alarm, what longing, what concern, what readiness to see justice done."

2. Community Healing: Restorative justice promotes the healing of relationships and the strengthening of community bonds, creating a more cohesive and supportive environment.

- Colossians 3:12-14: "Therefore, as God's chosen people, holy and dearly loved, clothe yourselves with compassion, kindness, humility, gentleness and patience. Bear with each other and forgive one another if any of you has a grievance against someone. Forgive as the Lord forgave you. And over all these virtues put on love, which binds them all together in perfect unity."

3. Enhanced Witness: A church that practices restorative justice serves as a powerful witness to the world,

demonstrating the transformative power of the gospel and the reality of God's kingdom.

- John 13:34-35: "A new command I give you: Love one another. As I have loved you, so you must love one another. By this everyone will know that you are my disciples, if you love one another."

Restorative justice, as outlined in 1st and 2nd Corinthians, offers a powerful framework for addressing harm and fostering reconciliation. By embracing these principles, individuals and communities can experience profound transformation, reflecting the heart of the gospel and the ministry of reconciliation entrusted to believers. The church, as the body of Christ, is called to embody these values, creating environments where justice, healing, and reconciliation thrive. Through this exploration, we have aimed to provide a comprehensive understanding of restorative justice as a vital aspect of Christian faith and practice, paving the way for a justice that truly embodies the heart of God's kingdom.

REFERENCES

- The Holy Bible, New International Version

- Various passages and teachings from the New International Version (NIV) of the Bible were referenced to explore the principles of restorative justice as outlined in 1st and 2nd Corinthians.

- Commentaries on 1st and 2nd Corinthians

- Garland, David E. 1 Corinthians. Baker Exegetical Commentary on the New Testament. Grand Rapids: Baker Academic, 2003.

- Hays, Richard B. First Corinthians: Interpretation: A Bible Commentary for Teaching and Preaching. Louisville: Westminster John Knox Press, 1997.

- Harris, Murray J. The Second Epistle to the Corinthians: A Commentary on the Greek Text. New International Greek Testament Commentary. Grand Rapids: Eerdmans, 2005.

- Barnett, Paul. The Second Epistle to the Corinthians. New International Commentary on the New Testament. Grand Rapids: Eerdmans, 1997.

- Books and Articles on Restorative Justice and Biblical Reconciliation

- Zehr, Howard. The Little Book of Restorative Justice. Intercourse: Good Books, 2002.

- Wright, N.T. Paul and the Faithfulness of God. Minneapolis: Fortress Press, 2013.

- Marshall, Christopher D. Compassionate Justice: An Interdisciplinary Dialogue with Two Gospel Parables on Law, Crime, and Restorative Justice. Eugene: Wipf & Stock, 2012.

- Braithwaite, John. Restorative Justice and Responsive Regulation. Oxford: Oxford University Press, 2002.

- Schrock-Shenk, Carolyn, ed. Making Peace with Conflict: Practical Skills for Conflict Transformation. Scottdale: Herald Press, 1999.

- Yoder, John Howard. The Politics of Jesus. Grand Rapids: Eerdmans, 1994.

- Volf, Miroslav. Exclusion and Embrace: A Theological Exploration of Identity, Otherness, and Reconciliation. Nashville: Abingdon Press, 1996.

- Kidder, David S., and Noah D. Oppenheim. The Intellectual Devotional: Revive Your Mind, Complete Your Education, and Roam Confidently with the Cultured Class. New York: Rodale Books, 2006.

- Weaver, J. Denny, ed. The Nonviolent Atonement. Grand Rapids: Eerdmans, 2001.

STUDY QUESTIONS FOR EACH CHAPTER

Chapter 1: Understanding Restorative Justice

1. How does restorative justice differ from retributive justice?

2. What biblical principles support the concept of restorative justice?

3. How can restorative justice be applied in everyday life?

Chapter 2: Context of 1st and 2nd Corinthians

1. What were the major social and cultural challenges in Corinth during Paul's time?

2. How did these challenges influence the issues Paul addressed in his letters?

3. How does understanding the historical context of Corinth help us apply Paul's teachings today?

Chapter 3: Restorative Justice in 1st Corinthians

1. How does Paul address division and factionalism in 1 Corinthians 1-4?

2. What steps does Paul outline for dealing with sexual immorality in 1 Corinthians 5?

3. Why does Paul criticize lawsuits among believers in 1 Corinthians 6?

Chapter 4: Restorative Justice in 2nd Corinthians

1. How does Paul urge the community to reconcile with a repentant offender in 2 Corinthians 2:5-11?

2. What is the "ministry of reconciliation" Paul describes in 2 Corinthians 5:11-21?

3. How do these teachings apply to conflict resolution in the church today?

Chapter 5: Practical Applications of Restorative Justice

1. What are some practical ways churches can implement restorative justice in their disciplinary processes?

2. How can restorative justice principles be applied to community life beyond formal disciplinary actions?

3. What challenges might arise when implementing restorative justice, and how can they be addressed?

Chapter 6: Building a Restorative Culture

1. Why is education important for building a restorative culture?

2. What role does leadership play in promoting restorative justice within the church?

3. How can supportive structures and policies enhance the implementation of restorative justice?

Chapter 7: Going from 2 Corinthians 5 to Romans 5

1. How does Paul's teaching in 2 Corinthians 5 emphasize the idea of not counting sins against offenders?

2. What are the implications of seeing individuals as new creations in Christ?

3. How does Romans 5 provide a theological foundation for reconciliation?

Chapter 8: The Ripple Effect of Restorative Justice

1. What is the "ripple effect" of harm and crime, and how does restorative justice address it?

2. How does the passage from Romans 5:20b highlight the power of grace in restorative justice?

3. What practical steps can be taken to implement restorative justice in a community?

Chapter 9: The Inbreaking of Divine Justice

1. How do Paul and the Gospel writers present God's justice as a redemptive power?

2. What role does radical forgiveness play in the kingdom of God?

3. How can these principles be applied to modern church practices?

Chapter 10: The Measure of Human Righteousness

1. What is contributory justice, and how does it differ from merit-based justice?

2. How does Paul's teaching in Ephesians 2 and other passages inform our understanding of justice?

3. What practical steps can churches take to embody contributory justice?

Chapter 11: New Testament Restorative Practices

1. How does Matthew 18 outline a process for resolving harms and offenses?

2. What is the significance of the "seventy-times-seven" forgiveness principle?

3. How can these principles be integrated into church and community practices?

Chapter 12: The Cruciform Nature of Restorative Justice

1. How does Paul describe the role of believers as ambassadors of reconciliation in 2 Corinthians 5?

2. What is the importance of vulnerability and re-empowerment in restorative justice?

3. How can the principles of restorative dialogue be practically applied?

Chapter 13: Ambassadors of Reconciliation

1. How does Paul's concept of believers as ambassadors of reconciliation inform our understanding of justice?

2. What are the key principles of restorative justice highlighted in 2 Corinthians 5:16-21?

3. How can these principles be applied in contemporary church and community settings?

Chapter 14: A Biblical Restorative and Retributive Justice

1. What are the key principles of restorative and retributive justice in 1 Corinthians 6:1-11?

2. How can these principles be integrated into the church and state justice systems?

3. What is the concept of "Biblical Gacaca," and how can it be implemented?

Discussion Guide for Small Groups

Introduction and Guidelines:

1. Set a welcoming and respectful atmosphere.

2. Encourage active participation and listening.

3. Ensure confidentiality and sensitivity to personal sharing.

Sample Discussion Guide:

Week 1: Understanding Restorative Justice

1. Share personal experiences or observations of justice in your community.

2. Discuss the differences between restorative and retributive justice.

3. Explore how biblical principles support restorative justice.

Week 2: Context of 1st and 2nd Corinthians

1. Discuss the social and cultural challenges in Corinth during Paul's time.

2. Reflect on how understanding this context helps in applying Paul's teachings today.

3. Identify similar challenges in your community and how Paul's guidance can address them.

Week 3: Restorative Justice in 1st Corinthians

1. Discuss how Paul addresses division and immorality in the church.

2. Reflect on the importance of internal conflict resolution.

3. Explore ways to apply these principles in your church.

Week 4: Restorative Justice in 2nd Corinthians

1. Reflect on the concept of the ministry of reconciliation.

2. Discuss the role of forgiveness and reconciliation in church conflicts.

3. Share ideas on implementing these teachings in your community.

Week 5: Practical Applications of Restorative Justice

1. Explore practical ways to implement restorative justice in church discipline.

2. Discuss how restorative principles can be applied in community life.

3. Identify potential challenges and solutions.

Week 6: Building a Restorative Culture

1. Discuss the importance of education and leadership in promoting restorative justice.

2. Reflect on how to create supportive structures and policies.

3. Share experiences of building a restorative culture.

Week 7: Going from 2 Corinthians 5 to Romans 5

1. Reflect on the implications of viewing people as new creations in Christ.

2. Discuss the role of grace in reconciliation.

3. Explore how these principles can transform your community.

Week 8: The Ripple Effect of Restorative Justice

1. Discuss the concept of the ripple effect and its impact.

2. Reflect on the role of grace in overcoming harm.

3. Share practical steps to implement restorative justice.

Week 9: The Inbreaking of Divine Justice

1. Discuss how Jesus' teachings on forgiveness and nonretaliation apply today.

2. Reflect on the transformative power of God's justice.

3. Explore ways to integrate these principles into church practices.

Week 10: The Measure of Human Righteousness

1. Reflect on the concept of contributory justice.

2. Discuss how to apply biblical principles of justice in daily life.

3. Share practical steps for embodying contributory justice.

Week 11: New Testament Restorative Practices

1. Discuss the process for resolving conflicts in Matthew 18.

2. Reflect on the significance of radical forgiveness.

3. Explore ways to integrate these principles into community practices.

Week 12: The Cruciform Nature of Restorative Justice

1. Reflect on the role of vulnerability and re-empowerment in justice.

2. Discuss the principles of restorative dialogue.

3. Share practical applications for these principles.

Week 13: Ambassadors of Reconciliation

1. Reflect on the role of believers as ambassadors of reconciliation.

2. Discuss key principles of restorative justice from 2 Corinthians 5:16-21.

3. Explore practical applications in church and community settings.

Week 14: A Biblical Restorative and Retributive Justice

1. Discuss the principles of restorative and retributive justice in 1 Corinthians 6.

2. Reflect on integrating these principles into justice systems.

3. Explore the concept of "Biblical Gacaca" and its implementation.

Additional Resources on Restorative Justice

- Books:

- Zehr, Howard. The Little Book of Restorative Justice. Intercourse: Good Books, 2002.

- Marshall, Christopher D. Compassionate Justice: An Interdisciplinary Dialogue with Two Gospel Parables on Law, Crime, and Restorative Justice. Eugene: Wipf & Stock, 2012.

- Wright, N.T. Paul and the Faithfulness of God. Minneapolis: Fortress Press, 2013.

- Braithwaite, John. Restorative Justice and Responsive Regulation. Oxford: Oxford University Press, 2002.

- Articles:

- Schrock-Shenk, Carolyn, ed. Making Peace with Conflict: Practical Skills for Conflict Transformation. Scottdale: Herald Press, 1999.

- Yoder, John Howard. The Politics of Jesus. Grand Rapids: Eerdmans, 1994.

- Online Resources:

- Center for Justice and Reconciliation: [www.restorativejustice.org] (http://www.restorativejustice.org)

- The International Institute for Restorative Practices: www.iirp.edu
- Restorative Justice Council: [www.restorativejustice.org.uk] (http://www.restorativejustice.org.uk)

These appendices provide additional support for individuals and groups seeking to understand and implement restorative justice principles in their communities, fostering environments of reconciliation, healing, and transformation.

220